In the Footsteps of
I.K.Brunel

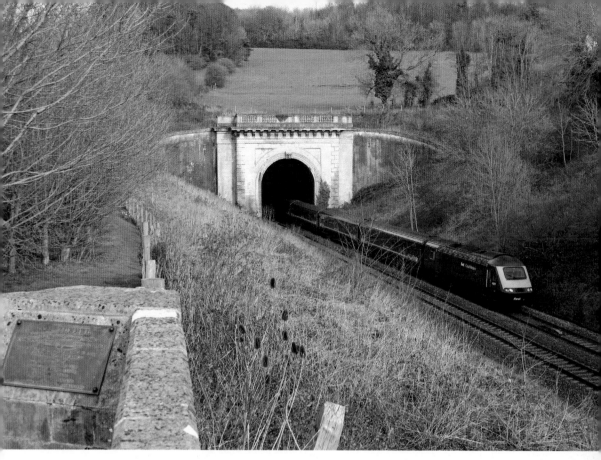

In the Footsteps of
I. K. Brunel

Jonathan Falconer

Ian Allan
PUBLISHING

First published in 1995 as *What's Left of Brunel*
This new edition published 2014

ISBN 978 0 7110 3798 4

Published by Ian Allan Publishing Ltd, Hersham, Surrey, KT12 4RG.

Printed in England

Visit the Ian Allan Publishing website at www.ianallanpublishing.com

Front cover top Royal Albert Bridge, Saltash. *Samut/Stockphoto*

Front cover bottom SS *Great Britain*. *National Maritime Museum*

Front cover inset This famous photograph of Brunel by Robert Howlett is perhaps the most characteristic and widely known portrayal of the great engineer. *(See page 10)*

Back cover In this view of c1906, Brunel's original iron swivel bridge over the South Entrance Lock in Bristol has been moved, but can still be seen a few yards away on the lock side adjacent to the North Entrance Lock. *(See page 85)*

Previous page The façades of Box Tunnel's two portals have altered little over the years. *(See page 65)*

CONTENTS

ACKNOWLEDGEMENTS

Since this book was first published in 1995 under the title of *What's Left of Brunel*, several previously overlooked examples of Brunel's work have been rediscovered. Much new information has also come to light as well as changes to the ways in which we can experience Brunel's legacy in the 21st century. Most notable, perhaps, has been the rediscovery and salvage of a previously unrecognised iron bridge by Brunel built over the canal at Paddington in West London in 1839.

Interest in Brunel and his engineering legacy remains strong, which has inspired this fully revised, updated and largely re-illustrated new edition to give readers an insight into the life and achievements of Isambard Kingdom Brunel, as well as the latest information (as at September 2014) about where his works can be seen today.

Acknowledgements to the original (1995) edition and this (2014) edition My grateful thanks go to the following individuals and institutions, whose collective help has been invaluable and indispensable in the writing of this book (names being listed alphabetically rather than in any particular order of merit): Helen Ashby, Curator of Collections, National Railway Museum, York; Associated British Ports, Plymouth; Bob Barnes, Honorary Secretary, Brunel Exhibition Rotherhithe; Bath Central Library; Bradford-on-Avon Library; Captain David Campbell, Plymouth City Harbourmaster; Mike Chrimes, Librarian, Institution of Civil Engineers, London; Crossrail Ltd, for permission to reproduce copyright photographs; Paul Elkin, Curator of Technology at Bristol Museum, for his critical appreciation of my original draft work on Brunel in Bristol; Friends of the General Cemetery Co, Kensal Green, London; Ian Black, Crossrail Ltd, Ken Brunt, Jon Godfrey, Maxwell Hamilton, The Rail Engineer online magazine, Frederic Sancho, Geof Sheppard, South American Pictures/Marion Morrison, US Library of Congress, Derek Webb, Wikimedia Commons (Andy Dingley, Neddyseagoon, Ed Webster) for their kind permission to reproduce copyright photographs; Guildhall Library, London; John Hughes, Local Studies Librarian, Swansea Central Reference Library, for his help with documentary sources for Briton Ferry Dock; The Illustrated London News, for kind permission to reproduce illustrations which appeared in various issues between 1843 and 1864; Nick Lee, Bristol University Library; Caroline Marais, of the Pumphouse Educational Museum, Rotherhithe; Cliff Morgan, for information on the present redevelopment of Briton Ferry Dock and for kindly supplying archive photographs for this section; Brian Morrison, transport photographer; Richard Mortimer, Keeper of the Muniments, Westminster Abbey, for his ready assistance with details of the Brunel memorial stained-glass window in the Abbey; Plymouth Central Library; Neil Sinclair, Senior Curator, Sunderland Museum & Art Gallery, for his help with documentary sources relating to Monkwearmouth Dock, Sunderland; SS Great Britain Trust, Bristol; Swansea Central Reference Library; Trowbridge Library; Tyne & Wear Development Corporation; and, last but by no means least, to my wife, Annie, for so valiantly putting up with my obsessive interest in all things Brunel.

Uncredited pictures are from the author's collection. Every effort has been made to trace the copyright holders of photographs, but in some cases this has not been possible. The author will be happy to hear from those with whom he has been unable to make contact.

INTRODUCTION

Just what is it that continues to set Isambard Kingdom Brunel apart from the other engineers of early Victorian England? Was it his more daring solutions to engineering problems, when others (like the Stephensons) moved cautiously for fear of upsetting their shareholders?

Or was it his highly innovative and artistic streak, characterised by his keenness to try every new device? Or perhaps it was his commitment to the highest technical excellence possible.

Whatever the reasons, Isambard Brunel's reputation as an engineering genius, forged in the crucible of 19th-century Britain's industrialisation, remains as solid today as it was 160 years ago. Yet the Brunel family, until fairly recently, looked upon Isambard's father, Sir Marc, as the more successful engineer and his son as a 'glorious failure'. How the passage of time has radically altered this viewpoint; civil engineers of the 21st century look upon Isambard as among the greatest of the Victorian engineers.

Isambard Kingdom Brunel, in an engraving made in 1858 from a studio photograph.

When, in the early-Victorian age, engineering acquired a professional status Brunel was one of the first of this new breed of multi-disciplined engineers who could turn their expertise to shipbuilding as easily as they could to railway- or bridge-building. However, this facility did not last for long, because the engineering profession was soon to fragment into the various specialisms of mechanical, electrical, maritime and the other disciplines we know today.

Born at Portsea in 1806, the son of a French émigré engineer and designer, Isambard Brunel went on to become one of the finest engineers of the Victorian era. His principal achievements over a 30-year period included the design and engineering of a sub-aqueous tunnel beneath the River Thames (in partnership with his father), three suspension bridges, three transatlantic passenger liners, the Great Western Railway line from London to Bristol, with all its numerous bridges, tunnels, cuttings, viaducts and stations, and a number of dock schemes of varying success. As the finest professional engineer of his time he was also in great demand on innumerable other projects as a consulting engineer, although his links with many of these were, at best, fairly tenuous.

Thankfully there is much that remains today of Brunel's achievements for us to appreciate, but there is also a significant proportion that has not survived into the 21st century. Notable amongst these are his steamships the *Great Western* and *Great Eastern*, the original Hungerford Bridge across the River Thames, the South Devon 'atmospheric' railway, numerous station buildings and the dozens of wooden viaducts in Cornwall between Plymouth and Penzance. For those structures that have survived it is not always a foregone conclusion that they will be protected by those set to watch over them from demolition or despoliation (see Chapter 8).

Perhaps the most enduring of all Brunel's achievements is the Great Western Railway, which links London with Bristol by 118 miles of iron railway track. His desire to provide the fastest and most comfortable journey west means we can enjoy the same standards of rail travel today along the very same trackbed that was surveyed and laid out more than 170 years ago. The only differences today, of course, are the advances in train and rolling-stock design, track construction and signaling, which allow line speeds in excess of 125mph to be achieved daily in complete safety and air-conditioned comfort, by the High Speed Trains that now hurtle along the line. Plans for electrification of the Great Western main line could mean even greater speeds and shorter journey times. This is a far cry from the much slower broad-gauge steam locomotives of the Victorian era, with their comparatively rudimentary carriages – open-topped for Third-class passengers.

In a more indirect way, the design and construction principles that Brunel applied to his shipbuilding ventures, the *Great Western, Great Britain* and *Great Eastern,* were subsequently adopted by shipbuilders the world over. Today they form the basis of the techniques now employed by many modern shipbuilders.

For our present-day society, which often wants more for less, Brunel's solutions to bridge-building problems are interesting. His breathtaking but structurally very strong designs, like the Clifton Suspension Bridge in Bristol, were made possible by a daring use of engineering dynamics to extract maximum structural performance from a minimum of materials.

Brunel shunned state honours as a mark of merit but believed in honour through the public recognition of his works. This he achieved, and we can still see and admire much of his work around us today.

The aim of this book is two-fold: first, to describe the achievements of Brunel, the great engineer, that remain today, relating why and how he built what he did, and, second, to show where those achievements can be seen. It is hoped that the book will appeal to a wide range of readers, including those with a general interest in Britain's industrial heritage, as well as history students studying the Victorian age at schools and colleges. A detailed gazetteer, listing what remains, where to find it and how to get there, is included towards the end of the book.

Finally, the facts and figures contained in these pages are, to the best of the author's knowledge, accurate and true. This pertains in particular to the gazetteer, where the telephone numbers and opening times of the attractions, and public transport serving them, can be found, but it is always advisable to double-check such details in advance of any visit, in order to avoid disappointment.

Jonathan Falconer
Bradford-on-Avon
May 2014

PART ONE

BRUNEL
THE MAN AND HIS
ACHIEVEMENTS

Brunel statue on the Paddington Station
concourse adjacent to Platform 1. *Author*

1   BRUNEL, THE MAN

Above This famous photograph of Brunel by Robert Howlett is perhaps the most characteristic and widely known portrayal of the great engineer. Hands in pockets and lighted cigar in the corner of his mouth, he stands before the massive launching chains of the PSS *Great Eastern* in November 1857.

Had it not been for the French Revolution, Britain might never have known its most successful and innovative engineer of the Victorian era.

His name was Isambard Kingdom Brunel. Compared with the engineering partnership of George Stephenson (1781–1848) and his son Robert (1803–59) and with the engineer Thomas Telford (1757–1834), Brunel's achievements were wider-ranging and transformed the face of Victorian England.

The achievements of the Stephensons and Telford were undoubtedly significant, but the legacy of Brunel's pioneering work lives on into the 21st century in the form of the Great Western Railway line from London to Bristol, notably his series of viaducts, bridges, tunnels and cuttings, as well as his work on docks and transatlantic ship design. All have positively influenced engineering practices and continue to touch the everyday lives of many Britons.

But what of the man behind the engineering successes? What were his personal qualities, as distinct from those required by his chosen profession? Before reviewing his life, some insights into his character will help to put his achievements into a clearer perspective.

Brunel was what we would today term a workaholic. He was also a lifelong insomniac; his diary entries, often made in the small hours of the morning whilst chain-smoking cigars, bear

silent testimony to this fact. Long hours and hard work were, to him, an unquestionable feature of his profession, and it was probably this unrelenting diet of hard work, nervous energy and little sleep, year in year out, that finally broke his health.

Although a family man, Brunel was very much wedded to his chosen profession and expected fellow engineers and assistants to share his burning enthusiasm and drive for a project, giving no quarter to those who failed to live up to his high expectations. But he was equally supportive of those assistants in his employ whom he perceived to be doing their job to the very best of their abilities. He observed – and expected from others – high standards of courtesy,

Above Brunel's engineering contemporaries of the Victorian age – Thomas Telford (*Above left*) and Robert Stephenson (*Above*). *The Illustrated London News*

Left Brunel was a workaholic. Here are some of the surveying instruments that he took with him in a travelling chest when working on site. In the foreground are a selection of his drawings and plans for Bristol docks, the PSS *Great Eastern* and his Great Western Railway stations. *Author*

personal conduct and integrity. Indeed some commentators have portrayed him as paternalistic and authoritarian towards his assistants, rather in the mould of a stern father of the early Victorian period.

Although Brunel was undoubtedly a great engineer, there were some less admirable sides to his character. A number of commentators have described him as being almost impossible to work with because he did not (or perhaps could not) delegate work easily or willingly. He was often unable to price a job accurately, and the large cost overruns that frequently followed caused anger amongst shareholders, contractors and bankers alike. His tendency to choose the most dramatic – rather than the most practical and cost-effective – solutions sometimes backfired on him, and he occasionally went a little bit too far beyond the bounds of technological development, the failed 'Atmospheric' railway scheme and his huge steamship, the *Great Eastern*, being sad and costly examples of these tendencies.

In common with many other men from all walks of Victorian commercial life Brunel believed strongly in the fundamental principle of British Liberalism in the 19th century, that of laissez-faire. He was very much against patent legislation as a means of protecting an individual's commercial rights and was implacably opposed to any form of state or government interference in the engineering profession.

With these character traits in mind, the pages that follow will reveal something of his tremendous achievements set within the context of Isambard Brunel as a real person rather than as a one-dimensional character from a history book.

Isambard's father, Marc Brunel, a Frenchman, was an inventor and engineer whose family had lived for more than 300 years in the little village of Hacqueville in Upper Normandy, midway between Rouen and Paris. However, as a Royalist Marc Brunel was forced to flee France for New York in 1793 to escape certain death at the hands of the revolutionaries. Later, in 1799, he re-crossed the Atlantic to England, where he married Sophia Kingdom and settled at Portsea, Portsmouth, which was close to his work interests of manufacturing wooden pulley blocks at Portsmouth Naval Dockyard. It was at the Brunels' small terraced house at No 1 Briton Street, Portsea, in the early hours of 9 April 1806 that Sophia gave birth to a son, Isambard Kingdom, the youngest of three children.

Isambard grew up in a cultured home environment and, thanks to the strong character of his father, received an excellent education, first at home and then at a number of small schools. Like many fathers at any point in history Marc was very keen for his son to do well and have better opportunities than he had had as a boy. He was also determined that his son should carve a distinguished career for himself as an engineer, and Isambard was steered by his father accordingly. Through careful tutoring at home and at school his youthful impetuosity was gradually tempered by a certain tenacity and exactitude when it came to problem-solving, and an imaginative artistic flair soon characterised his many designs.

In 1820 Isambard was sent to France in order to improve his mathematical education, at the College of Caen in Normandy and at the Lycée Henri-Quatre in Paris. To the casual observer Isambard's olive complexion and lively dark eyes, combined with his tendency to gesticulate in conversation, often made him appear more French than English. He spent a useful period as an apprentice to Louis Breguet, a respected maker of chronometers, watches and scientific instruments, before returning to England and his family in August 1822, at the age of 16.

Isambard now began to work for his father (who was busy on designs for a number of bridges and commercial docks in Britain and France) from his small office at No 29 Poultry, in the City of London. By this stage it was obvious to Marc that his son was developing into a gifted engineer.

In July 1825 Marc Brunel was appointed engineer of a new and ambitious scheme to drive a tunnel under the River Thames between Rotherhithe and Wapping – a daring feat of engineering for the time and one that would later be described by *The Illustrated London News* as 'the seventh [sic] wonder of the world'. When both Marc and his deputy became ill in April 1826 Isambard was thrown into the daunting role of resident engineer, but he proved himself to be eminently capable of managing the difficult operation and was later confirmed in the position under his father.

The actual task of digging beneath the Thames was achieved by using Marc Brunel's unique cast-iron Tunnelling Shield (*see page 29*), which enabled 36 drill operators to work back-to-back with bricklayers whilst the tunnel roof was supported by the iron frames of the shield. In common with earlier attempts to tunnel under the Thames the Brunels' effort was plagued with many problems, culminating in a catastrophic breach of the tunnel and a flood on 12 January 1828, which claimed the lives of several labourers and almost killed Isambard. After this tragic episode work on the tunnel was abandoned until 1836 and was not completed until 1843.

During his convalescence, Isambard's attentions became focused on the West of England, at Bristol, where designs had been invited for an iron suspension bridge to span the Avon Gorge at Clifton. Of the 20 designs submitted in 1829 four were by Isambard Brunel. The Bridge Committee appointed Thomas Telford as judge, and, perhaps predictably, he rejected all the designs, proposing instead his own less impressive solution of twin Gothic piers rising from the bottom of the gorge to support a triple-span suspended deck. Public opinion was not altogether in favour of this solution, however, and wisely the Bridge Committee announced a second competition in 1830. Of the 12 designs submitted Isambard Brunel's was judged the best, and in March 1831 Brunel was formally appointed Engineer to the Clifton Suspension Bridge.

Brunel's winning design was for a single-span suspension bridge to straddle the gorge, measuring 702ft between the two piers, which were constructed on stone abutments set into the gorge on either side. The deck was suspended from a series of iron rods and chains 245ft above the level of high water in the River Avon below (*see page 103*). Work on the construction of the Clifton-side pier began in June 1831 but was suspended in October following the Bristol Riots. The bridge was plagued by financial troubles throughout the

Right Brunel's elegant Hungerford suspension bridge, opened on 1 May 1845. *The Illustrated London News*

protracted period of its construction, and it was not until 1864, five years after its creator's death, that it was formally opened to traffic.

Similar in appearance to the Clifton design was Brunel's Hungerford Bridge, spanning the River Thames in London between Lambeth and Hungerford Market, today the site of Charing Cross station. The central span of this pedestrian suspension bridge measured 676ft between the two piers, which were built to an Italianate design. Opened to the public in May 1845, Hungerford

Isambard Kingdon Brunel – time chart

9 Apr 1806	Born at Portsea, Portsmouth, son of Marc Brunel
Apr 1820	Begins studies in France at Caen College and Lycée Henri IV, Paris
21 Aug 1822	Returns to England and works for his father
Jan 1827	Appointed Resident Engineer on the Thames Tunnel, London
12 Jan 1828	Badly injured in accident in Tunnel
1829	Submits four designs for suspension bridges across the Avon Gorge, Bristol; Telford rejects all four
1830	Submits winning entry in second competition for suspension bridge
10 Jun 1830	Elected Fellow of the Royal Society
Jun 1831	Work begins on Clifton Suspension Bridge, Bristol
Oct 1831	Work on Clifton Suspension Bridge suspended following Bristol Riots
1831/2	Work on Thames Tunnel abandoned
Feb 1833	Plans to modernise Bristol Docks implemented
7 Mar 1833	Appointed Engineer of the Great Western Railway (GWR)
1835	Work begins on Monkwearmouth Dock, Sunderland
Aug 1835	GWR Bill receives Royal Assent
29 Oct 1835	Proposal for 7ft broad-gauge rail sanctioned
Jul 1836	Marriage to Mary Horsley
28 Jul 1836	PS *Great Western*'s keel laid down at Bristol
27 Aug 1836	Work resumes on Clifton Suspension Bridge
1837	Monkwearmouth North Dock opens for trade
19 Jul 1837	PS *Great Western* launched at Bristol
1837	Injured in accident aboard PS Great Western
1838	Work begins on Bristol Temple Meads station
Apr 1838	PS *Great Western*'s maiden voyage to New York
Jan 1839	Appointed Engineer to the South Devon Railway (SDR)
19 Jul 1839	SS *Great Britain*'s keel plates laid down at Bristol

Isambard Kingdon Brunel – time chart (continued)

31 Aug 1840	Bristol Temple Meads station completed
30 Jun 1841	GWR line open throughout for traffic from London to Bristol
25 Mar 1843	Tunnel opens to the public
19 Jul 1843	SS *Great Britain* launched at Bristol
1844	Appointed Engineer of the broad-gauge South Wales Railway
1845	Work begins on South Entrance Lock to Bristol Docks
1 May 1845	Hungerford Bridge, London, opens for pedestrian use
26 Jul 1845	SS *Great Britain*'s maiden voyage to New York
May 1846	First section of SDR opens using 'Atmospheric Traction'
13 Sep 1847	'Atmospheric' trains carry passengers between Exeter and Teignmouth
1848	'Atmospheric' experiment on SDR abandoned
April 1848	Preliminary work begins on Royal Albert Bridge at Saltash
Apr 1849	South Entrance Lock to Bristol Docks opens to traffic
1849	Construction begins on Brunel's designs for Paddington New Station
12 Dec 1849	Sir Marc Brunel dies aged 81
Jul 1852	Chepstow Bridge opens to traffic across River Severn
1853	Work begins on Briton Ferry Dock, South Wales
1853/4	Lack of funds stops work on Clifton Suspension Bridge
Jan 1853-Sep 1857	Supervises construction of Royal Albert Bridge
16 Jan 1854	Paddington New Station opens (departure side)
Jul 1854	PSS *Great Eastern*'s keel plates laid down at Millwall
1 Feb 1855	World's first postal train runs from London to Bristol
16 Feb 1855	Asked to design transportable temporary wooden hospital buildings for British Army in Crimea
12 Jul 1855	Hospital at Renkoi, Crimea, ready to accept patients
3 Nov 1857	First launch of PSS *Great Eastern* attempted
31 Jan 1858	PSS *Great Eastern* launched at Millwall, East London
May 1859	Royal Albert Bridge opens to traffic
9 Sep 1859	PSS *Great Eastern* suffers boiler explosion on sea trials
15 Sep 1859	Isambard Kingdom Brunel dies at 18 Duke Street, London, aged 53
20 Sep 1859	Buried at Kensal Green Cemetery, London
Jun 1860	PSS *Great Eastern* makes first Atlantic crossing
22 Aug 1861	Briton Ferry Dock officially opens
8 Dec 1864	Clifton Suspension Bridge officially opens

Achievements of three of Brunel's engineering contemporaries

Thomas Telford (1757–1834)

Ellesmere Canal (1793–1805)

Caledonian Canal (1803–23)

Gotha Canal between Baltic Sea and North Sea (1808–10)

Birmingham & Liverpool Junction Canal (1825–34)

Menai Suspension Bridge, Anglesey (1826)

Conway Bridge, North Wales (1826)

Tewkesbury Bridge (1826)

Gloucester Bridge (1828)

Dean Bridge, Edinburgh (1832)

Bridges at Glasgow and on River Clyde (1829–34)

Aqueducts over Ceiriog Valley at Chirk (1796–1801) and Dee (1795–1805)

Bridges over River Severn at Montford and Buildwas

St Katherine's Dock, London (1826–8)

Harbours including Wick, Aberdeen, Peterhead, Banff, Leith and Dundee (1796–1834)

London–Holyhead road (fully open 1826)

Almost 1,000 miles of new roads in northern counties of Scotland

Approximately 120 bridges

Drainage of large tracts of Fenland (1818–34)

42 Highland churches (1824–34)

George Stephenson (1781–1848)

Ellesmere Canal (1793–1805)

Built colliery locomotive *My Lord* (1814)

Locomotive engine with steam-blast patented (1815)

Invented Colliery Safety Lamp contemporaneously with Humphrey Davy (1815)

Engineer to Stockton–Darlington Railway, first public railway to use steam traction

Engineer to Liverpool & Manchester Railway (1824–30)

Prize-winning locomotive *Rocket* (1829)

Robert Stephenson (1803–59)

Ellesmere Canal (1793–1805)

London–Birmingham Railway line (1833–8)

High Level Bridge, Newcastle (1849)

Britannia Bridge, Anglesey (1850)

Victoria Bridge, Berwick (1850)

Montreal Bridge, Canada (1859)

Brunel chronology – parallel events

1805	Nelson defeats combined French and Spanish fleets at Trafalgar
1806	Napoleon crushes Prussian Army at Battles of Jena and Auerstadt
1815	Napoleon defeated in Belgium at Battle of Waterloo by British and Prussian forces
1818	Mary Shelley publishes her novel Frankenstein
1819	Peterloo Massacre in Manchester
1820	Liberal revolt begins in Spain
1821	John Constable's painting 'The Hay Wain' shown at Royal Academy, London
1829	Catholic Emancipation Bill enacted in England
1832	English Reform Bill extends voting rights
1833	Oxford Movement formed within Church of England to restore High Church ideals
1834	Tolpuddle Martyrs prosecuted and transported for forming branch of Labourers' Union Abolition of slavery in the British Empire Thomas Telford, engineer, dies
1837	Victoria accedes to the British throne John Constable dies
1839	Artist Paul Cézanne born in France W.H. Fox Talbot's first photographic negative
1840	'Penny Post' introduced in Great Britain
1844	J.M.W. Turner paints 'Rain, Steam and Speed'
1845	Potato Famine in Ireland
1846	Corn Laws repealed
1847	10-Hours Act limits hours of work for women and children in all British industries
1848	Second French Republic proclaimed Engels and Marx publish 'Communist Manifesto' George Stephenson, engineer, dies
1851	J.M.W. Turner dies Great Exhibition held in London
1852	Napoleon III establishes Second French Republic
1853	Sir George Cayley's glider makes successful manned flight
1853	Gustav Courbet paints 'The Bathers'
1854	Crimean War begins Charles Dickens publishes Hard Times
1855	Paris Exhibition
1856	Bessemer introduces new method of steel processing
1859	Charles Darwin publishes On the Origin of Species Robert Stephenson, engineer, dies

Bridge enjoyed a brief life, being dismantled in 1862, although the suspension chains were reused for the Clifton Suspension Bridge.

In 1832 Brunel turned his problem-solving mind from matters above water to those below, having been recruited by the Bristol Docks Co in 1832 to report on the problems of silting and water flow in the city's floating harbour. However, the over-cautious dock company implemented only a few of his recommendations, and it was not until 1840, when the matter of silting in the harbour had got worse, that Brunel was asked to report again. By 1842 the company was forced by the dire circumstances to adopt his sensible suggestions, which involved dredging the harbour and the construction of new culverts and a new entrance lock (*see page 85*). Further north, during the same period Brunel designed a new dock at Sunderland for the Monkwearmouth Dock Co. Known as the North Dock, it was built between 1835 and 1837 but was destined never to be a great success. However, Brunel's involvement with the design and construction of the Briton Ferry Floating Dock, near Neath, in South Wales, begun in 1853 but not opened until 1861, two years after his death, proved more commercially successful in the long term. Due mainly to its more advantageous location, a thriving trade in both coastal and export traffic continued to bring prosperity to the dock until well into the 20th century. At 50ft, the large wrought-iron semi-buoyant dock gate which Brunel designed for Briton Ferry was, at that time, the widest single-span dock gate in existence.

In 1830s and '40s the petty wranglings between Brunel and the Bristol Docks Co were needless distractions from the greater works he was about to embark upon. In August 1835 the Great Western Railway Bill received Royal Assent, and the Great Western Railway (GWR) was empowered to build a railway line from London to Bristol, with Brunel as Engineer. Over the ensuing six years and at the height of 'railway mania' 118 miles of railway line – arguably the finest and most enduring of Brunel's many engineering achievements – were laid between Paddington and Bristol, passing through Maidenhead, Reading, Swindon, Chippenham, Box and Bath. The work proceeded contemporaneously from London and Bristol and involved the construction of innumerable cuttings, bridges, viaducts, tunnels and, of course, stations, of which Paddington New (1849–54) and Temple Meads (1840) were the two most significant examples, built in the neo-Tudor/Gothic architectural house style of the GWR. The line was opened to the first through trains on 30 June 1841, and, thanks to the gentle curves

Above Paddington station, gateway to the West of England and South Wales. The Great Western Railway is probably Brunel's most enduring achievement. *Author*

and shallow gradients adopted, Brunel's 'billiard table' remains eminently suited to the high-speed trains of today (*see page 46*). During the 1840s Brunel's engineering skills were equally in demand on the continent of Europe. He was appointed as engineer to the Genoa–Turin railway, which was built during this period by the Sardinian government and included the two-mile Giovi Tunnel, which passes underneath the Ligurian Apennine mountain range.

With regard to the GWR, Brunel himself could see that the opportunities for convenient and comparatively rapid travel derived from his London–Bristol railway line need not end at Bristol, for the construction of a transatlantic steamship would enable passengers to travel onward to New York, which would thus be reached in record time. The seeds of this solution were sown in 1836 with the formation of the Great Western Steamship Co, with Brunel as a member of the design committee. The keel of the world's first ocean-going steamship was laid down the same year, and on 19 July 1837 the *Great Western,* as she was known, was launched from the Wapping Dock at Bristol. She sailed for New York on 8 April the following year, completing the outward journey in 15 days 10 hours instead of the usual 36 days taken by sailing packets.

Another first for Brunel in the world of maritime engineering was his iron-hulled screw-propelled steamship, the *Great Britain*, a vessel of even greater proportions than her predecessor. Her keel plates were laid down at Bristol in July 1839, and she was floated in the Great Western dry dock on 19 July 1843, duly making her maiden voyage to New York in July 1845. Her maximum speed of around 12 knots surpassed even that of the fastest paddle-steamers of the day.

Amidst all his great schemes for bridges, tunnels, railways and ships Brunel still found time for romance and courtship. After a two-month engagement he married Mary Horsley on 5 July 1836. The daughter of William and Elizabeth Horsley, Mary came from a strongly artistic and musical background, not dissimilar to that of her husband, and her family home in Kensington often received visits from the eminent composers of the day, notably Brahms, Mendelssohn and Chopin. In spite of her background Mary showed little artistic flair herself but provided her husband with a stable and comfortable home life and three children – two sons, Isambard and Henry Marc, and a daughter, Florence Mary. Neither son fathered any children, and the male line of the Brunels ultimately died out, although the name was retained by Florence as part of her married name.

Returning to *terra firma*, Brunel now turned his problem-solving genius to the construction of another railway, the South Devon Railway (SDR), which was planned to link Exeter with Plymouth. The severe gradients likely to be experienced along its steep and winding route led Brunel to question the ability of existing locomotives to cope. His solution, proposed in 1844, was to adopt a principle, developed and patented several years earlier by the Samuda brothers, which became known as 'Atmospheric Propulsion'. Put simply, this involved the laying of a 15in cast-iron pipe between the rails through which a piston was drawn by a partial vacuum, propelling the railway carriage to which it was attached along the line above, with no need for a locomotive. Technical problems eventually caused Brunel to concede defeat, and the experiment was abandoned in 1848, although 'atmospheric' passenger-carrying trains had first run between Exeter and Teignmouth in September the previous year.

In 1848 preliminary work had begun on Brunel's last and most spectacular example of bridge building, the Royal Albert Bridge at Saltash. With an overall length of 2,200ft, the double-span, single-track iron bridge, supported mid-river by a central iron and stone pier, provided a rail link across the River Tamar between Devon and Cornwall. For financial and technical reasons construction work did not begin in earnest until 1853, and when the bridge was finally opened to traffic, on 3 May 1859 by Prince Albert himself, Brunel was not present due to growing ill health.

A project less readily associated with Brunel's popular image was his involvement in 1855, at the behest of the War Office, with the design of a wooden prefabricated Army hospital to be shipped to the Crimean peninsula on the Black Sea. Here British forces under the command of Lord Raglan had since March 1854 been fighting alongside those of France in defence of Turkey against Russia. Bureaucratic incompetence in London and the appalling insanitary conditions at the military hospital in Scutari led to a public outcry at home, thanks mainly to the revealing reports in *The Times* newspaper by William Howard Russell and the activities of the British nurse Florence Nightingale. Brunel's design for the hospital was for a simple unitary construction, each unit consisting of two wards, each ward accommodating 24 patients complete with self-contained toilet and washing facilities, ventilation fans and nurses' quarters. By virtue of its construction this temporary hospital could be expanded simply by bolting on additional units as and when required. Having received the initial request in February 1855, Brunel had designed and shipped the prefabricated sections to Renkoi in the Crimea by July; the hospital was fully operational and receiving its full quota of patients by December. The guiding principles of unitary construction used by Brunel at Renkoi have since become standard practice in the design of prefabricated structures.

Whilst the Crimean War continued to hold the attention of the British press and public, work began in July 1854 on Brunel's third and final great steamship design, the *Great Eastern* (originally to be known as the *Leviathan*). Intended to incorporate many of the latest design features of the day, she was more than twice the length of the *Great Britain*, eight times the displacement and featured the very latest in iron-hull design and construction; indeed the construction methods employed by Brunel in his iron-hulled ships were improved upon in later years only by the adoption of steel and by better welding and joining techniques. The propulsion offered by the *Great Eastern*'s twin steam engines was novel in that they powered two paddle-wheels and a screw propeller. Because of her great length she was built parallel to the Thames riverbank at Millwall, in East London, the intention being to launch her sideways. However, a combination of the seemingly inevitable financial problems (which beset so many of Brunel's projects), a poor working relationship with John Scott Russell, the builder, and a number of abortive attempts at launching meant that the *Great Eastern* finally took to the river for the first time on 31 January 1858. On 9 September 1859, while on her initial sea trials in the English Channel off Portland, she suffered an explosion in her engine room which caused serious damage and six deaths amongst the crew but fortunately did not cause her to sink. Following repairs the *Great Eastern* had a sadly lacklustre career which saw her confined to laying cables across the North Atlantic between Britain and the USA and also in the Indian Ocean, ending her days as a floating bazaar on the River Mersey.

Concurrent with his heavy involvement in the building and launch of the *Great Eastern* Brunel was engaged in drawing up designs for the East Bengal Railway in India. However, his pressing work commitments at home and his fragile state of health prevented him from visiting the works during their construction.

By now Brunel was a very sick man, having suffered a stroke on 5 September whilst already weakened by an acute kidney infection. He died at his home in Duke Street, London, on 15 September 1859, aged 53, and was buried alongside his mother and father in the family tomb at Kensal Green Cemetery in North West London – appropriately within earshot of his Great Western Railway line from Paddington.

Left The enormous *Great Eastern* (seen here at New York) became Brunel's nemesis. It was largely down to the stresses of finance and personality clashes with his partner and builder of the ship, John Scott Russell, that Brunel became ill and died.

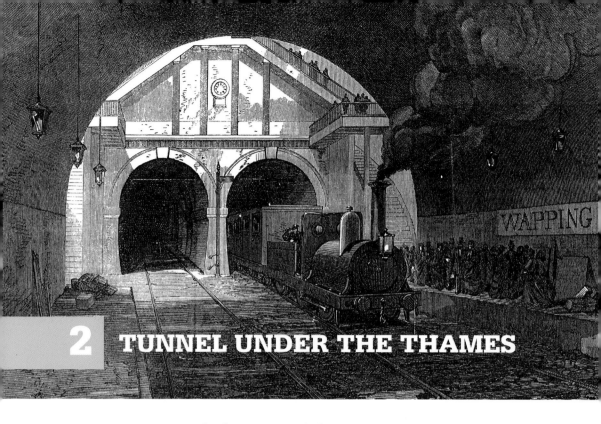

2 TUNNEL UNDER THE THAMES

At the beginning of the 21st century there are 23 tunnels crossing under the River Thames, these being used for a variety of purposes including Tube and railway lines, road transport and utilities.

When the latest tunnel to be constructed is completed in 2018 it will deliver Crossrail train services between Plumstead (on the south side) and North Woolwich on the north bank. This new Thames tunnel will be cut about 50ft below the existing riverbed (the Brunels' tunnel is just 15ft) and will be 1.6 miles long. Until the mid-18th century there were only two ways of moving people or goods across the Thames in London – taking them across London Bridge or putting them in a boat. There were no tunnels under the river at that time. Although another river bridge was opened in 1750 at Westminster, to be followed by 1817 by six more, upstream from London Bridge, only one was built close enough to relieve the horrendous traffic jams on London Bridge. With the huge and rapid expansion of London as a port, shipping congestion on the river grew, the situation being compounded by the 350 or so ferries that plied the river each day and the 4,000 or more carts and carriages that daily clogged up the roadway on London Bridge. The need was soon recognised for another river crossing – above or below the water

Above A northbound train on the East London line draws to a halt at Wapping station, shortly after the opening of the line through the Thames Tunnel in 1869.
The Illustrated London News

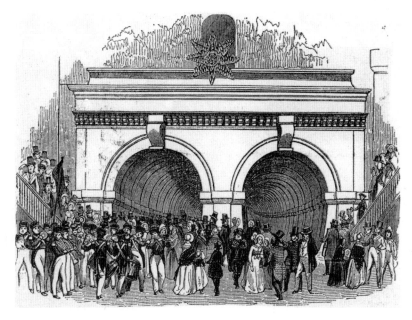

Left The Thames Tunnel was reached via long stairways from surface level down through the brick tunnel shafts to the tunnel entrances below. The long climb was not very popular with the pedestrians who used them between 1843 and 1869, there being more than 100 steps at Rotherhithe and 99 at Wapping, This is the surface-level entrance to the tunnel at **Wapping.** *The Illustrated London News*

– that would help relieve the chronic congestion around London Bridge and in the east of the city.

In July 1825 Marc Brunel was appointed engineer of a new and ambitious scheme to drive a tunnel under the Thames between Rotherhithe and Wapping. The spot chosen was between London Bridge and Greenwich, 4 miles downstream, where such a crossing could be attempted without hindering the great mercantile enterprises on both sides of the river. However, two previous attempts at tunnelling under the Thames had been abandoned as impracticable, and Marc Brunel's bid, assisted by his son Isambard, would be a daring feat of engineering for their time if they managed to pull it off.

Below The Thames Tunnel and its environs.

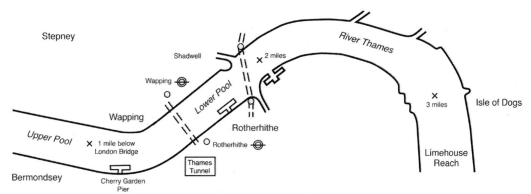

Marc Brunel's attempt to tunnel under the Thames was certainly not the first, for in 1799 Ralph Dodd, engineer of the Grand Surrey Canal, proposed a 2,700ft-long tunnel between Gravesend and Tilbury, some 24 miles downstream from Rotherhithe. Work was begun but abandoned very soon afterwards. The second attempt was made by Cornish engineer Robert Vazie, assisted by Richard Trevithick, who proposed a driftway tunnel under the river from Rotherhithe to Limehouse, preparatory to constructing the tunnel proper alongside. Work on the 1,200ft-long tunnel commenced in 1805, but on 26 January 1808, 200ft short of the north shore, the tunnel suffered a catastrophic flood, and the directors of the Thames Archway Co lost their nerve, abandoning the scheme soon afterwards.

Perhaps it was a case of third time lucky when the Thames Tunnel Co received Royal Assent on 24 June 1824 and Marc Brunel was appointed engineer. However, work on the 1,140ft-long tunnel would nearly bankrupt Marc and almost kill both him and Isambard. To begin with, on 2 March 1825, the first bricks of a huge brick cylinder, 40ft high and 50ft in diameter, were laid, on a 25-ton iron hoop above ground on the Rotherhithe bank, braced by iron tie-rods and rings. The brick cylinder was excavated from within and beneath so that it would gradually sink into the ground under its own weight at the rate of 6in a day, thus forming a secure shaft from which the tunnelling operation could be mounted. Excavations continued downwards for a further 20ft, and the walls of the shaft were faced with brick, leaving an aperture 36ft wide facing north to accommodate the Tunnelling Shield, of which more anon.

By 6 June the 1,000-ton cylinder had sunk to its full depth, the shaft was underpinned, and the iron rings removed. A superstructure and platform were now constructed on top of the cylinder, on which was assembled a stationary steam engine, used to pump up water from inside the shaft and to remove spoil from the bottom of the workings. A sump was constructed beneath the shaft to collect water draining from the workings; once work was underway this would then be pumped to the surface by a more powerful steam engine housed next to the shaft. The crowns of the twin tunnel arches were to be just 14ft beneath the bed of the Thames at its deepest point.

Marc Brunel had devised a highly innovative method of digging beneath the riverbed using his unique cast-iron Tunnelling Shield. This bulky piece of equipment, composed of 12 huge cast-iron frames each measuring 21ft 4in high, 3ft wide and 6ft deep from front to back, rested on the floor of the tunnel on cast-iron feet. Similar feet, known as staves, held up the roof of the workings

Below The Rotherhithe entrance to the tunnel. *The Illustrated London News*

above each frame. Six of these frames were used in each of the twin tunnels, and each frame was divided into three levels, forming a total of 36 work areas along a common working face. Each work area was manned by a single excavator and, when fully manned by 36 miners, who worked in two eight-hour shifts, this permitted a tunnel face of about 800sq ft to be excavated. At the front of each frame a tier of heavy oak planks, known as 'poling boards', were held firmly against the face by two jacks, or 'poling screws'. Each workman removed one poling board at a time and excavated behind it with a pick and shovel to a depth of just 4½in, replacing the poling board afterwards and securing it with the extended poling screws. This laborious process was repeated in each frame until all the ground had been excavated; then the entire frame was moved forward by 4½in by means of horizontal screw jacks, in much the

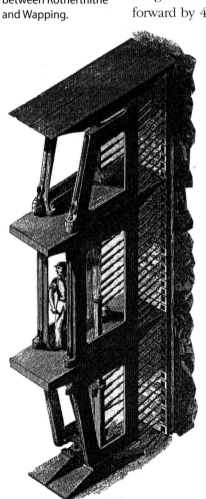

Below Revolutionary for its time, the iron Tunnelling Shield was designed by Marc Brunel to excavate the 1,200yd-long tunnel beneath the Thames between Rotherthithe and Wapping.

same manner as a car jack works today. All the poling screws were then retracted, and the excavation procedure began again.

Bricklayers worked back-to-back with the excavators to complete the job, so the whole tunnel was continuously supported except for the 4½in where the frame had just been moved forward. The tunnel's brick lining, for which a special high-strength 'Roman' cement was used, was at least 2ft 6in thick throughout. A wheeled timber stage followed behind the bricklayers, with the dual task of supplying them with materials and removing spoil from the excavations. The Tunnelling Shield was fully installed and operational on 28 November 1825, and during the first few months of tunnelling an average of 200 men at a time were employed on the whole undertaking.

When both Marc and his deputy, John Armstrong, fell ill in April 1826 Isambard became resident engineer by default but proved himself to be eminently capable of managing the difficult operation, at times working solidly for 36 hours at a stretch. On his return Marc appointed three assistants – Richard Beamish, William Gravatt and Francis Riley – to aid his overworked son, who, as of 3 January 1827, at the age of 20, had now been confirmed in the position of resident engineer under his father.

Right The dual processes of tunnelling and bricklaying can be readily appreciated from this annotated cutaway drawing of the shield in place inside the tunnel.

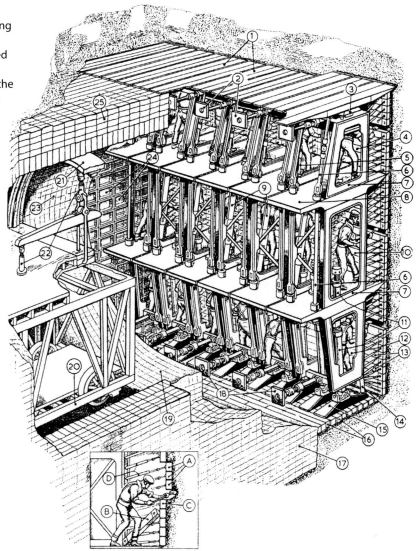

1: Top staves
2: Top abutting screws
3: Head
4: Top box of frame No 6
5: Tail jack
6: Wrought-iron reducing member
7: Cast-iron side frame member
8: Upper floor plate of frame No 6
9: Sling
10: Middle box of frame No 6
11: Leg
12: Bottom box of frame No 6
13: Poling boards
14: Jack forcing down floorboards
15: Shoe
16: Floorboards on which brick roadways rest
17: Brickwork of dividing wall
18: Bottom abutting screws
19: Brick roadway
20: Travelling stage
21: Roof centring
22: Jacks for adjusting roof centring
23: Western side-wall
24: Side staves
25: Roof brickwork
A: Poling board moving forward
B: Poling board removed so that miner can excavate
C: Poling board that has not been moved forward
D: Poling screws

Work in the tunnel was hard and dirty, with the constant danger of the tunnel's collapsing and flooding from the Thames overhead a distinct possibility. Waterborne diseases like cholera from the filthy river claimed the lives of many miners working in the tunnel, including that of Francis Riley. This fear did nothing to prevent the tunnel company's directors from allowing frequent visits to the workings by dignitaries and members of the public, much to the alarm of Marc Brunel, who was all too well aware of the dangers; later in the tunnel's construction, 34,000 people visited the tunnel workings during the course of 1839, whilst receipts from visitors for the year ending March 1841 amounted to £1,705 – representing a vain attempt by the directors to recoup some of the huge investment in the tunnel.

On 8 May 1827 the excavators broke into a large hole in the riverbed, created by gravel dredging, and in this, the first of several major floods, the tunnel was completely filled with foul river water. Using a diving bell borrowed from the East India Docks Co, Isambard descended into the murky waters of the Thames to inspect the breach on the riverbed. Having assessed the damage, he ordered that a bed of iron rods be laid across the breach and 150 tons of clay in sacks be placed over the top. It took three weeks to seal the hole before it was possible to start the lengthy process of pumping the water out of the tunnel, and almost six months would elapse before it had been pumped dry and tunnelling work could resume. In a bid to restore the faith of the Thames Tunnel Co directors, the workforce and the general public in the integrity of the tunnel Marc Brunel organised a somewhat unusual banquet, to be held under the river in the tunnel workings. In addition to the 50 or so distinguished guests and 120 miners and bricklayers who had been invited, the band of the Regiment of the Coldstream Guards played to the gathering by the golden light of four huge candelabra.

Barely eight months after the first breach, on 12 January 1828, the filthy waters of the Thames invaded the tunnel for a second time, killing six men and sweeping away Isambard. In little more than 15 minutes the entire length of the 600ft tunnel was under water. Isambard had been working in the shield at the time of the incursion and by sheer good fortune had been swept down the tunnel and about 40ft up into the tunnel shaft, to relative safety, although he sustained trauma to his leg, as well as internal injuries; six miners were not as fortunate and either drowned in the flood or were crushed under the wooden stage behind the shield. The ill health

Isambard was to suffer for the rest of his life may in part be attributable to the foul waters of the Thames, which at that time was little better than an open sewer. While Isambard recovered at Brighton from his serious injuries Marc Brunel descended in the diving bell to assess the damage on the riverbed. It was far more severe than the earlier breach and required more than 4,000 tons of clay to seal it. Pumping began on 21 January, and repair work proceeded until well into the summer, but in August a shortage of funds prompted the directors to order that the tunnel and the shield be bricked up, until further notice. An enormous mirror was then mounted on the wall at the end of the tunnel, to give the impression of a continuous archway.

After an interval of seven years Parliament finally sanctioned a loan to the Thames Tunnel Co, allowing the work to resume. Following a major clean-up operation in the tunnel workings and the installation of a new and heavier Tunnelling Shield, work recommenced, and by the end of 1836 an average headway of 4ft per week was being achieved. But within the space of the next seven months, on 23 August and 3 November 1837 and 20 March 1838, the tunnel suffered three more serious breaches, with the loss of one man's life. After successive repairs to the tunnel roof and pumping operations to clear floodwater, work continued very slowly, with the health of much of the workforce suffering badly from the ill-effects of the noxious air in the tunnel.

When the tunnel reached the low-water mark on the Wapping shore on 22 August 1839 the end of the titanic undertaking was

Below There were connecting arches between the twin parallel tunnels at regular intervals along their length. Here also can be seen something of the ceremony that accompanied the tunnel's opening in 1843. *The Illustrated London News*

almost in sight. However, money problems continued to plague the endeavour, and it was not until 16 November 1841 that the miners in the shield finally struck the red brick of the newly sunk Wapping tunnel shaft. Its days of usefulness now past, the great Tunnelling Shield was dismantled and brought to the surface where, contrary to the wishes of both Marc and Isambard, it was sold for scrap to help pay off the huge loan on the tunnel, realising the then not inconsiderable sum of £900.

Inside the tunnel, work proceeded on the finishing touches in anticipation of the first foot passengers: paving was laid, the tunnel walls were tiled, and permanent stairways and landings were constructed in the shafts, where the walls were whitewashed.

Below The tunnel was used as a pedestrian thoroughfare, as shown in this contemporary engraving, but in time it became the haunt of vagabonds and low-life. *Copyright unknown*

Chronology of work on the Thames Tunnel

March 1825		The formal opening of work on the Rotherhithe shaft
November 1825		Boring of the tunnel begins
September 1826	260ft	
January 1827	350ft	Isambard is appointed as Resident Engineer
March 1827	470ft	
May 1827	547ft	first major flood
November 1827		Celebration banquet is held in the tunnel, work resumes
January 1828	605ft	second major flood, six men killed, Isambard injured; work is abandoned
August 1828		Tunnel face bricked-up but tunnel is still open for viewing by visitors
March 1835		New shield is installed and tunnelling restarts
1836	713ft	
August 1837	736ft	third major flood
September 1837		Tunnelling restarts
November 1837	741ft	fourth major flood, one miner killed
March 1838	763ft	fifth major flood
1838	821ft	
August 1839	920ft	low-water mark is reached on Wapping shore
1839	1,015ft	
March 1840		Marc Brunel is knighted by Queen Victoria
1840	1,091ft	(76ft in two months)
June 1840		Brunel takes possession of land for the Wapping shaft
January 1841	1,140ft	tunnel is completed to breadth of the river
November 1841	1,200ft	shield reaches the Wapping shaft
August 1842		Western arch on the Wapping side opens
March 1843		Tunnel officially opens to the public

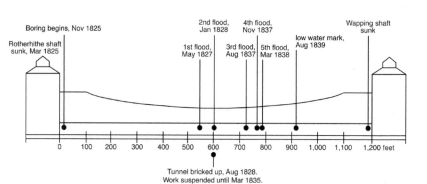

Left The main events in the construction of the Thames Tunnel, 1825–43.

Crossrail – a new Thames tunnel for the 21st century

A link with the first Thames tunnel built by Marc and Isambard Brunel has found expression in the ambitious 21st-century Crossrail construction project in London.

Work began in 2009 to cut the Crossrail tunnels under London in what is Europe's largest railway and infrastructure construction project. The main civil-engineering construction works are planned to complete in 2017 with fitting out of stations and testing to follow. Passenger services are due to start in 2019. The Crossrail network will operate a fleet of 650ft-long trains, each capable of carrying 1,500 people, along a 73-mile railway line connecting the City, Canary Wharf, the West End and Heathrow Airport to commuter areas east and west of the capital.

The main feature of Crossrail is the 26 miles of new tunnels bored by eight state-of-the-art Tunnel Boring Machines (TBMs). They will run from near Paddington station in the west to Stratford in the east, via Central London and Liverpool Street station. An almost entirely new line will branch from the main line at Whitechapel in East London to Canary Wharf, crossing the River Thames, with a new station in Woolwich and connecting with the North Kent line at Abbey Wood, in South East London.

Crossrail has used eight TBMs to construct the 26 miles of new tunnels under the streets of London. The giant machines have carefully navigated subterranean London around the entwined networks of the capital's Tube tunnels, sewers, utilities and hidden rivers, at depths of up to 130ft.

The specially built 1,000-ton, 500ft-long TBMs are the modern-day equivalents of Marc Brunel's Tunnelling Shield. They are underground factories that not only cut tunnels but also remove the spoil and create a sealed concrete tunnel behind them as they go. Each machine has a rotating cutter head at the front; behind, a series of trailers houses all the mechanical and electrical equipment needed for the excavation of material. The giant machines drill at an average rate of more than 300ft a week, installing pre-cast concrete segments as rings to form the tunnel lining as it advances forwards. Each TBM is operated by a 'tunnel gang' of 20 – 12 on the TBM itself and eight working between the rear of the machine and the surface.

Right Crossrail's Tunnel Boring Machines (TBMs) have been operated in pairs to deliver the east- and westbound tunnels for each of the tunnel drives. In keeping with tunnelling tradition the machines were given names. The pair used to construct the tunnel between Plumstead and North Woolwich (the only point where the Crossrail route passes under the River Thames) were named *Mary* and *Sophia*, in tribute to the wives of Isambard and his father Sir Marc Brunel. *Crossrail Ltd*

Above *Sophia* was the fifth TBM to complete factory testing. This is her cutting face. To help reduce the chance of settlement while the tunnels were constructed, the TBMs were run for nearly 24 hours a day, seven days a week, 365 days a year, although there were scheduled breaks to allow for maintenance on the TBMs. *Crossrail Ltd*

Right A construction worker inspects the completed tunnel beneath the River Thames. The TBMs drilled at an average rate in excess of 300ft a week, installing pre-cast concrete segments as rings to form the tunnel lining as it advanced forwards. *Crossrail Ltd*

Left Concrete segments 1.6m (5ft 3in) wide have been used to create the permanent tunnel walls. To allow for the tunnel's curvature the segments differ in shape. *Crossrail Ltd*

The cost of building a Thames tunnel

BRUNEL, 1837

(Estimated cost, 1825: £160,000)

£180,000 of company's capital expended

£84,000 of Exchequer bills advanced by Government

Total   £264,000

(Actual cost for completion, 1837: £614,000)

£150,000 to complete tunnel

£200,000 for shaft on Wapping side and proposed circular approach roads

Grand Total £614,000

(Data source: The Illustrated London News, 1 April 1843)

CROSSRAIL, 2014

The anticipated cost of the entire Crossrail construction project is £14.2 billion.

On 7 November 1842 Marc Brunel suffered a stroke which paralysed his right side, but fortunately he had recovered sufficiently to attend the official opening of the tunnel, on 25 March 1843.

Like many other pioneering efforts down the years the Thames Tunnel blazed a trail but failed to realise its principal objective of relieving heavy traffic congestion in the vicinity of London Bridge and in the City of London. Plans to build a pair of circular approach roads for carriage access came to nothing, and so died any hope of the tunnel's becoming a profitable concern and a palliative to the problems of traffic congestion. For a while it was used as a pedestrian thoroughfare, but it soon became the domain of tatty market stalls, while by night it was taken over by prostitutes and muggers, who lurked in the shadows of its many arches.

Following discussions about its future, on 25 September 1865 the Thames Tunnel was sold to the East London Railway for the sum of £200,000 – less than half what it had cost to build. Track was laid, improvements were made in order to bring it up to specification for rail traffic, and on 7 December 1869 the first passenger-carrying underground train passed through the tunnel, following which it served faithfully as a subaqueous link in the capital's Underground network until 1997, when the entire East London Line was closed for three years to allow essential repair work to the Thames Tunnel.

In December 2007 the tunnel was closed again, for track-laying and re-signalling of the East London Line extension. When it reopened in April 2010 it was as part of the London Overground

network, being now used once again by main-line trains. What was once the stub East London Line has now metamorphosised into the London Overground, creating new routes linking destinations north and south of the river as part of an orbital railway – in effect a kind of outer Circle Line.

What's left today?

As explained earlier, nothing is left today of Marc Brunel's great iron Tunnelling Shield; it was sold for scrap once the tunnel had been completed. Happily, the Thames Tunnel itself survives to this day as part of the London Overground rail network. Wapping and Rotherhithe are two intermediate stops on the London Overground East London Line which runs south from its terminus at Highbury & Islington via Whitechapel and Shadwell to Clapham Junction, Crystal Palace and West Croydon. It is possible to travel through the tunnel on one of the many trains that cross under the Thames each day.

Wapping station, on the north bank of the river, was built on the site of the original tunnel shaft, inside which were installed the

Above Used today by London Overground trains, the Brunels' Thames Tunnel has lost much of the grandeur that surrounded its early life, its fine portals being now barely visible behind all the paraphernalia of modern railway operations. This view of the tunnel portals at Rotherhithe shows well the proportions of the tunnel entrance. Together the twin tunnels measure 38ft wide, and each is 22ft 6in high. *Frederic Sancho*

passenger lifts that descend to platform level. Standing at the southern end of the platform it is possible to see the twin arches of the tunnel as they disappear beneath the river. In the station entrance hall can be seen a commemorative plaque to the Brunels and their achievement in building the Thames Tunnel. It was erected in 1959 by London Transport to coincide with the centenary of Isambard Brunel's death.

South of the river, **Rotherhithe station** was built a short distance to the south of the original tunnel shaft (which is used today as an inspection shaft for the railway below by London Underground engineers). The area to the north of the station is a conservation area which includes the old tunnel shaft, Brunel's Engine House and the Brunel Museum.

The **Brunel Museum**, a registered charity, is based at the Brunel Engine House in Railway Avenue, a stone's throw from the London Overground station at Rotherhithe. It was formed in 1973 as the Brunel Engine House & Museum to ensure that the achievements of the Brunels in the Thames Tunnel received proper recognition. The derelict Brunel Engine House, originally built by Marc Brunel to contain boilers which provided the power to drain the tunnel workings, gained Listed status (Grade II) and grants from the Department of the Environment to help with renovation work, together with financial help from the London Borough of Southwark, the erstwhile Greater London Council and the Docklands Development Team to secure the long-term viability of the project. Since then grants and assistance from a variety of official and private sources have enabled the Brunel Engine House and its museum to flourish.

Opposite The interconnecting arches inside the tunnels can be clearly seen in this photograph taken during work in 2009 for track-laying and infrastructure improvements.
Frederic Sancho

'GOD'S WONDERFUL RAILWAY'

'Railway mania'

Above Daniel Gooch
(1816–89) became
Brunel's locomotive
superintendent at the
Great Western in 1837,
and later its chairman.
Many of his designs
were built for the
GWR at the company's
Swindon Works after
it opened in 1843. The
'Iron Duke'-class 4-2-2
broad-gauge express
passenger locomotive
Lightning pictured here
was designed by Gooch
(seen on the footplate)
and built at Swindon.
Note the 8ft-diameter
driving wheels.

Before we look at Brunel's involvement in the design and construction of the Great Western Railway between 1835 and 1841 – dubbed 'God's Wonderful Railway' by an unknown commentator – it is worth considering some of the economic and social factors which led to the 'railway mania' of the first half of the 19th century.

The network of canals that had begun to spread across the country from the mid-18th century and the growing improvements in the standards of roads were simply not enough to meet the rapidly growing demands of British industry The blossoming effect of the industrial revolution that had begun in the 1740s provided the right conditions during the 1830s in terms of technological know-how and availability of materials – notably the use of iron for construction purposes and the development of steam propulsion – for a new mode of transportation to be developed. This was to be the railway.

So it was that railway building took off, soon reaching truly manic proportions. Today it is very easy for us to underestimate the scale of this undertaking, but to early Victorian society it was a monumental achievement, dwarfing all other public works schemes in terms of its modernity and scale; it was almost on a par with the building of Egypt's Great Pyramid several millennia before.

During the second quarter of the 19th-century railways were seen as an essential means of improving communications between towns and cities and the expanding of trade in many other sectors of the British economy This period also saw the backbone of the British railway system laid down, although much of the work was done after 1830 and especially in the boom years 1835–40 and 1844–8. By the end of the latter period 5,120 miles of railways were open for traffic.

Those who built the railway lines were faced inevitably with a number of difficulties, not least from the conflicting interests of turnpike trusts, coaching and canal companies. Physical, technical, political and financial problems also had to be faced. Unlike many other countries, capital for railway building in Great Britain was raised without any State assistance and the State devolved all direction and planning of the railways on to private individuals. In the earlier phase of railway construction, during the 1830s, a great deal of manipulation and bribing in Parliament by those with railway interests took place.

The railway boom in Great Britain, 1835–50

(*Cumulative totals of track opened in miles*)

Year	Miles	Year	Miles
1825	27	1841	1,775
1830	98	1842	1,939
1832	166	1843	2,044
1833	208	1844	2,236
1834	298	1845	2,530
1835	338	1846	3,136
1836	403	1847	3,876
1837	540	1848	5,129
1838	742	1849	5,940
1839	970	1850	6,559
1840	1,498		

Capital authorised for railway building prior to 1844 amounted to £83,848,000, and up to 1848 another £267,284,000 was authorised. Anyone with an eye to cashing in on the railway boom and who

Right The arms of the Great Western Railway, combining those of the cities of Bristol and London, adorn the entrance to Paddington station. *Author*

DOMINE·DIRIGE·NOS   VIRTUTE·ET·INDUSTRIA

had money to spare – from industrialists to cotton spinners, bank clerks to clergymen – invested in the railways. Many fortunes were made, while other speculators over-extended themselves and lost everything. This great burst in promotion and speculation on the railways – 'railway mania' – peaked in August 1845, when GWR shares bought at £80 reached £236; they then fell to £154 by the end of October and £144 at the end of November.

The costs per mile in Great Britain for building a railway line were very high in comparison with overseas railways, averaging £40,000 per mile. Once initially hostile landowners woke up to the fact that the railway line destined to carve its way across their fields actually increased land values, their appetites were whetted for high compensation sums and remained so. On the GWR the cost per mile in land and compensation was almost £6,700; on the London to Brighton line nearer £8,000.

Of course, a proportion of this national average of £40,000 per mile went on wages, purchases of land and materials, Parliamentary lobbying and bribes, and the often high costs inflicted on companies by their chief engineers. For men like Brunel, the railway boom was an engineer's dream as all manner of elaborate constructions in the forms of bridges, viaducts, tunnels and ornate stations were required.

The railway encouraged urban growth, industrial expansion, and served as an accelerator for the new and developing engineering skills needed by an increasingly industrialised economy. This huge economic stimulus had an added bonus, coming at just the right time to help pull Great Britain out of the worst economic slump of the 19th century in 1841/2.

Brunel and the Great Western Railway

Following a meeting of businessmen and civic leaders held at Bristol on 21 January 1833 it was resolved that a rail link to London was urgently needed if Bristol was to compete successfully with its trading rival, Liverpool. A route survey was commissioned, and from a number of candidates for the post Brunel was chosen as Engineer to what was soon to become known as the Great Western Railway.

Together with his assistant, W.H. Townsend, Brunel made a detailed survey over a three-month period of the proposed route for the line, covering much of the distance on foot and horseback in an exacting work schedule. Finally, on 31 August 1835, after much battling against rival interests in Parliament, the Bill for the GWR received the Royal Assent. Without any prior experience of railway building Brunel began work on arguably one of the most challenging and socially far-reaching civil-engineering projects of the Victorian era.

At this point a short digression is necessary. Brunel's desire to establish the GWR as the fastest and most comfortable railway led him to adopt what became known as the broad gauge, measuring

Below Despite strengthening of the roof and realignment of platforms and track, Brunel's Paddington New Station remains much as he designed it in the 1850s. Today HSTs and 'Adelantes' (pictured) have taken the place of the Great Western's broad-gauge 2-2-2 steam engines of the Victorian era.
Brian Morrison

Right A GWR broad-gauge 4-2-2 locomotive heads an express in Sonning Cutting over mixed-gauge track in the early 1890s.

Below The rather bleak frontage of the first Paddington station in Bishop's Road, opened in 1838. *The Illustrated London News*

7ft ¼in. His persuasive argument for the broad gauge was that it could accommodate more powerful engines pulling larger, more stable carriages at higher speeds. Although this gauge may well have suited the virtually flat run from London to Bristol with its gentle curves, other engineers, notably the Stephensons on the Stockton & Darlington Railway, had adopted the narrower (standard) gauge of 4ft 8½in, which Parliament decreed in 1845 as the standard for any new public railway. For a man such as Brunel, who was used to winning his case, this must have been a sore blow, both professionally and personally. Thereafter his broad gauge GWR was at odds with most of the country's railways, but it was not until 1892, nearly 40 years after his death, that the GWR finally abandoned the broad gauge.

Returning to the building of the GWR, construction began simultaneously from the London and Bristol ends. The civil engineering work westwards from London was comparatively light compared to that experienced at the Bristol end, with the obvious exceptions of Wharncliffe Viaduct, the Thames bridges and the cuttings at Sonning and Purley. The 11½-mile stretch from Bristol to Bath alone required five major bridges, seven tunnels (two of which were opened out in 1894), two viaducts and an embankment.

The first completed section of line ran westwards from a temporary terminus at Paddington, London, to Taplow near

Below In its original state the 891ft-long Wharncliffe Viaduct was built to a width of 30ft and carried two broad-gauge tracks, but in common with many other structures along the route it was altered in the 1890s to accommodate four parallel tracks. Seven miles from Paddington, the viaduct is the largest brick construction along the 118-mile route of the GWR from London to Bristol.
Maxwell Hamilton

Above Gentle curves and almost imperceptible gradients characterised Brunel's Great Western. The nickname 'Brunel's billiard table' derives from the line's gradient profile, which for almost 70 miles of the route does not exceed 1 in 1,320 and for the rest not more than 1 in 600, clearly shown in this photograph of the main line west of Swindon.
Brian Morrison

Maidenhead, Berkshire, and opened to the public on 4 June 1838. Seven miles from Paddington, between Ealing and Southall, the line passes over the eight semi-elliptical arches of Wharncliffe Viaduct, at 890ft from end to end the largest brick structure on the London–Bristol line. Between Taplow and Maidenhead the line crosses over the River Thames on the graceful twin-span Maidenhead Bridge, believed still to have the longest unsupported brick arches ever built. Each semi-elliptical arch spans 128ft but rises only 24ft 6in to the centre. Brunel's critics were convinced that such flat arches could not possibly stand for long but after a year they were still very much in place and remain so to this day.

The section from Maidenhead to Twyford was the next to be completed, on 1 July 1839, and Twyford served as the railway's western terminus until the troublesome Sonning Cutting was completed to link up with Reading in March 1840. Originally conceived by Brunel as a tunnel through Sonning Hill, the cutting is almost two miles long and varies in depth from 20ft to 60ft. Both Brunel and his contractors failed to appreciate the sheer scale of the work involved in blasting and digging some 7,800cu ft of rubble for each foot of length. Work was held up by the most appalling winter weather, which turned the unfinished cutting and much of the line before it into a quagmire. The contractor William Ranger was dismissed, and Brunel took charge of operations in a frantic effort to keep work on schedule. At one point some 1,200 navvies and 196 horses were working like Trojans, shifting more than 660,000cu ft of spoil per week.

From Reading the line was extended to Steventon, following the River Thames before heading north and crossing the river twice on multi-span brick arch bridges at Basildon and Moulsford (1 June 1840), and thence to Faringdon Road (later known as Challow), west of Didcot (20 July 1840). Hay Lane, 2½ miles southwest of Swindon, was the next section of line to be opened to the public, on 17 December 1840, that through to Chippenham following on 31 May 1841.

The 13-mile section between Chippenham and Bath was the most troublesome of the westbound operation, involving as it did the construction of a 270ft six-arch viaduct west of Chippenham station followed by a two-mile embankment and the monumental excavation several miles further on of the 9,636ft Box Tunnel (*see page 63*). Deep cuttings and embankments, a crossing over the River Avon at Bath, the diversion of the Kennet & Avon canal on the eastern approaches to the city at Sydney Gardens followed by another viaduct, were all required to complete the Herculean task.

Below On the eastern approach to Bath, at Sydney Gardens, Brunel diverted the Kennet & Avon Canal a mode of transport that was soon supplanted by the railway *Author*

Chronology of the building of the GWR, 1835–41

Section	Mileage from Paddington	Date opened to traffic
LONDON PADDINGTON	0	Commenced September 1835
Taplow	22.38	4 Jun 1838
Twyford	31.01	1 Jul 1839
Reading	35.78	Mar 1840
Steventon	56.42	1 Jun 1840
Faringdon Road	63.66	20 Jul 1840
Hay Lane	80.20	17 Dec 1841
Chippenham	93.76	31 May 1841
Bath Spa	106.70	31 Aug 1840
BRISTOL TEMPLE MEADS	118.28	Commenced September 1835

(*Line opened throughout on 30 June 1841*)

Meanwhile, the equally difficult section from the GWR's western terminus at Bristol Temple Meads station to Bath was eventually opened to traffic on 31 August 1840 after major civil-engineering work which included the building of five bridges, seven tunnels and two viaducts. With the troublesome Box Tunnel finally completed, the line was opened throughout from London to Bristol on 30 June 1841, at a total cost of over £6.5 million. In 2014 values this equates to about £19.8 billion (see www.measuringworth.com).

What's left today?

Although now more than 170 years old, the main line from London to Bristol is still very much alive and well and follows the same route laid down by its creator. There have been the inevitable improvements over the years to upgrade the safety and reliability of both the track and signalling to facilitate the operation of High Speed Train (HST) services, but the basic Brunelian design features remain unassailable.

Journey times then and now (Exeter express)

Station	Distance (miles)	Time, 1845	Time, 2014
Paddington	0	09.30	09.30
Didcot Parkway	53	10.43	10.11
Swindon	77	11.20	10.30
Bath Spa	107	12.10	10.59
Bristol Temple Meads	118	12.30	11.15
TOTAL JOURNEY TIME:		3hr	1hr 45min

The 118-mile train journey from Paddington to Bristol Temple Meads is fast and comfortable, with passengers travelling in air-conditioned carriages which are a far cry from the early rolling stock which Brunel would have known. The shallow gradients and wide sweeping curves incorporated by Brunel in his original plans for the GWR allow for a fast and efficient rail service today.

The table reproduced opposite provides a comparison of typical journey times in 1845 and 2014 between Paddington and Bristol Temple Meads.

Brunel's Great Western stations

Compared to other engineers of his time Brunel was unusual in extending his remit to include the design of station buildings and engine sheds. The influence of the GWR's neo-Tudor architectural house style spread from the stations and engine sheds along the length of Brunel's 'billiard table' to colour the architecture of a number of associated railways along the route.

Classification of GWR stations

Principal	One-sided	Minor
Paddington	Slough	Ealing
Didcot	Reading	Hanwell
Swindon		Southall
Chippenham		West Drayton
Bath		Taplow
Bristol Temple Meads		Twyford
		Pangbourne
		Goring
		Wallingford (Moulsford)
		Steventon
		Faringdon
		Shrivenham
		Hay Lane (temp)
		Wootton Bassett
		Corsham
		Box
		Saltford
		Keynsham

In his book *The History and Description of the Great Western Railway* (1846) J.C. Bourne classifies the 26 stations built on the line between London and Bristol from 1838 to 1844 as principal stations, one-sided stations, and second-class or minor stations. These are as follows:

Paddington

Paddington's first terminus station, in Bishop's Road, was opened on 4 June 1838 but proved to be somewhat inadequate for the job. It initially comprised a single wooden island platform beneath a wooden arched truss roof, open at the sides. Two more platforms were added before 1840 for arrivals, and the original platform was then used for departures. In 1850, realising that a new station was desperately needed, the directors of the GWR sanctioned the design of a new station by Brunel, assisted by the architect Sir Matthew Digby Wyatt, who had also worked with him on the railway village at Swindon.

Below The central span of Brunel's breathtaking wrought-iron and glass roof at Paddington. *Author*

Built in the right-angle between Praed Street and Eastbourne Terrace, the new station offered 10 lines of broad-gauge track and four platforms, covered overall by a triple-arch wrought-iron and

Left Much of the elegant architectural detailing at Paddington station is the work of Brunel's partner, Sir Matthew Digby Wyatt. *Author*

glass roof supported from underneath by two internal rows of cylindrical columns. Joseph Paxton, who had designed the impressive iron and glass Crystal Palace for the Great Exhibition of 1851, strongly influenced Brunel in his design treatment of Paddington new station. It was the first station to utilise Paxton's system of ridge-and-furrow glazing over the central half of each span, the outer portions being clad in galvanised iron. Digby Wyatt was largely responsible for the elegant ornamental architectural treatment of the station building.

The departures side of the station, adjacent to Eastbourne Terrace, opened to passenger traffic on 16 January 1854, the

Above Set into the wall at the head of Platform 1 is this plaque that commemorates the centenary of Paddington station in 1954. *Author*

arrivals side following five months later. Once completed, the new station formed an impressive iron-and-glass gateway to Great Western territory.

In Praed Street the trainshed is hidden behind the magnificent frontage of the Great Western Hotel (later to be called the Great Western Royal Hotel but known today as the Hilton London Paddington), designed in the French Renaissance style of Louis XIV by Philip C. Hardwick and opened on 8 June 1854 by Prince Albert the Prince Consort and the King of Portugal. The high mansard roof between prominent corner towers gives the impression of a French château. When opened it was the largest hotel in Britain, with 112 bedrooms and 15 sitting rooms, along with various lounges, public rooms and restaurants. Much of the fine external decoration, by John Thomas, was removed in the refurbishment of 1936–8, along with the original Hardwick interiors, which were replaced by the contemporary art-deco style. Today it boasts 364 guest rooms, including 28 suites.

Right Philip Hardwick's magnificent Great Western Royal Hotel is the frontage to Brunel's Paddington station, gateway to the West of England. *US Library of Congress*

What's left today?

Since its opening the station building and its associated structures have been modified. These alterations have included extension of the station offices (1881), construction of additional departure (1885) and arrival platforms (1893) and further platforms (1916), more extensions to the platforms, a new concourse and new east-side offices (1930-4), ironwork reinforcements or replacements, track realignment and improved signalling. A major renovation of the triple arches of the trainshed roof was undertaken and the concourse refurbished in the late 1990s, but the essence of Brunel's original station design and the Great Western Royal Hotel remains to this day.

Swindon

An article in *The Illustrated London News* of 18 October 1845 described Swindon station in glowing (although hardly objective) terms: 'The Railway station, or stations – for there is one on each side of the road – are, perhaps, second to none in the kingdom; and their accommodation is of the most elegant and splendid description. Independent of the magnificent Refreshment Rooms, on each side of the line, there are an excellent Hotel and sleeping apartments: they communicate with each other by a covered passage over the railway.'

In common with Chippenham, Swindon was the other principal station on the GWR line between London and Bristol not built with an overall roof.

Below When the GWR let the management of the hotel, dining and railway refreshment rooms at Swindon station to a local hotelier on a long-term contract it agreed to all regular trains stopping there for 10 minutes. For years afterwards the company tried to evade this clause, which caused unnecessary complications to its train timetabling. This engraving of Swindon station, showing clearly the over-bridge connecting its hotel and dining room, appeared in *The Illustrated London News* of 18 October 1845. *The Illustrated London News*

What's left today?

Swindon station now consists of a single island platform reached by means of a subway under the line. The original passenger station building and hotel were demolished to allow redevelopment of the new station building.

Swindon Railway Village

During the early 1850s Brunel decided to build some 300 terraced cottages and other amenities for the employees of the GWR, south of the railway line at Swindon. Working in conjunction with architect

Right Designed by Brunel and Digby Wyatt in the 1850s, these solidly built railwaymen's cottages in Swindon's Railway Village narrowly avoided demolition in the 1960s. *Author*

Below One of three pubs in the Railway Village which still provides for spirituous needs of the locals. *Author*

Above Chippenham was classified by J.C. Bourne in his *The History & Description of the GWR* (1846) as one of the four principal stations on the GWR main line between the termini at London and Bristol. *Author*

Below Immediately to the west of Chippenham station a substantial bridge and viaduct carries the main line across the busy junctions of the A4 and A429 roads. *Author*

Sir Matthew Digby Wyatt, Brunel's desire to provide reasonable living conditions for the GWR's workforce resulted in a development of two blocks of three parallel rows of cottages, separated by wide streets with names such as Bristol Street and Bathampton Street. In the central section of the village, between the two flanking sets of terraced streets, was a main square in which was built the GWR Mechanics' Institute where evening classes in a variety of core subjects were held for the benefit of the workers and their families. A market, three pubs and a church were also built to cater for the nutritional, spirituous and spiritual needs of the community.

What's left today?
During the 1960s the Railway Village came close to being demolished to make way for the inevitable office and shop development. Thanks to the intercession of Swindon Borough Council who purchased the freehold of most of the cottages from British Rail, the village has been renovated and its character preserved. Today the village is very much alive and the houses are still lived in, one of which has been restored as a museum piece to show how a typical house in the village would have looked in Brunel's day. A hostel built by the GWR in 1854 on the corner of Faringdon Road, and which subsequently became a Wesleyan Chapel, housed the former Great Western Railway Museum.

Chippenham

Only the forebuilding (not the platform structure) is believed to date from the 1840s.

Bath Spa

In common with Temple Meads station, Bath Spa shares a common neo-Tudor/Gothic style. This architectural treatment of the station building and the castellated entrance to the viaduct at the western end of the station has received much criticism from architectural pundits over the years. This is hardly surprising when one considers the predominantly Georgian architectural style of buildings in the city. However, if one bears in mind the lack of sentiment displayed by a notoriously sentimental Victorian society to demolish structures that did not fit in with their views on architectural revival, or which stood in the way of progress,

Left Brunel favoured a Tudor/Gothic architectural styling for many of his stations and viaducts. This is the castellated centrepiece of St James's Viaduct, on the western approach to Bath Spa station. *Author*

Left At Bath Spa station passengers enter the building at ground level and climb stairs to reach the departure platforms on the first floor. *Author*

then the incongruity of the designs is not surprising at all. Echoes of this attitude can also be found in British town planning of the 1960s and '70s.

What's left today?

Although Brunel's overall hammer beam roof to Bath station was removed at the end of the 19th century, the station building still retains many of its original architectural features. Today, access to the platforms can be gained by a stairway from the booking hall for the up platform, and via a subway and stairs for the down side. The station concourse was tidied up in the late 2010s and now offers an attractive pedestrianised open space adjacent to the main station building.

Bristol Temple Meads

Right The 184ft-long frontage of the original Temple Meads terminus faced west onto Temple Street. Bourne describes its appearance thus: 'The centre is of three stages, with a principal doorway, and above it an oriel window, common to two stories, battlemented above, flanked by a window on either side between two buttresses. These buttresses are panelled towards the front and ascend nearly to the parapet. The centre is terminated by two octagonal turrets, which rise clear of the parapet. This part of the parapet is embattled and pierced with open work, excepting over the oriel, where it is a solid raised compartment, bearing the armorial ensigns of the Company.'
Author's collection

The original Temple Meads terminus survives today as the oldest railway terminus in the world to preserve most of its original shape and layout. Work began in 1838 on the station's offices fronting the street, and the whole station building was completed and opened to the public on 31 August 1840. Its frontage in Temple Gate was built in the GWR's grandiose neo-Tudor/Gothic house style, behind which were constructed a series of massive brick arches to support the engine and trainsheds. In the vaults beneath the rail tracks, Brunel planned stables, waiting rooms and storage facilities. A mezzanine floor above the engine shed supported on iron columns housed the Company's drawing office.

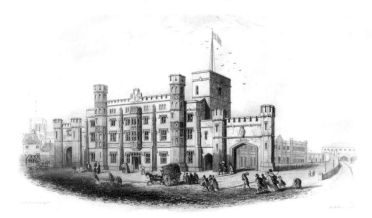

BRISTOL TERMINUS, GREAT WESTERN RAILWAY.

By the time of its completion in 1840 the station boasted an impressive 74ft single-span hammer-beam roof covering the 220ft-long trainshed, which spanned five broad-gauge tracks and was linked to the railway company's neo-Tudor offices that fronted onto Temple Gate. In the central portion of the building's frontage, the station superintendent lived on the top floor, the GWR Board Room

Left The battlemented top of the station still bears the arms of the GWR, although the ravages of time and pollution have left their mark on the stone. *Author*

Below The same view today. The central portion of the building is little changed apart from the obvious signs of weathering to the soft Bath stone, but the clock has long since gone, and the wing to the right was demolished in 1878 to build the approach ramp to the enlarged Temple Meads station. *Author*

Above The wings on the left and right of the main frontage contained archways for carriages, along with a side gate for passengers arriving on foot. Above the left portal was a clock. *Author*

and passengers' ticket office occupied the first floor, while the company clerk lived on the ground floor. Sandwiched between the station's offices and the huge trainshed, beyond the arrivals platform and beneath a vented roof, was an area with two running tracks where engines could draw forward and stand after being uncoupled from their trains. It was here that the engines were coaled and ashes could be thrown down chutes between the tracks to pits beneath the station arches. Water for the boilers was supplied from an elevated tank in the left-hand corner of the station.

Passengers arrived by coach or on foot and entered the station's precincts through the left-hand portal before ascending a staircase to reach the platform above the basement level. Coach traffic then passed to the right underneath the platforms and lines to make its exit through the right-hand portal.

In 1845 a separate terminus was built at right-angles to the first station building, for use by the Bristol & Exeter Railway, followed by an Express Curve platform to link the two termini. However, work began on plans for a new principal station for Bristol with the passing of the Bristol Joint Station Act in 1865. Financial disagreements between the three companies (GWR, MR, B&ER) delayed the completion of the new station until 1878 when a huge iron tied-arch roof over the Express Curve platform was designed by Francis Fox and a new down platform was built opposite this; Brunel's original terminus was extended, almost doubling the platform lengths; and a neo-Tudor booking hall and refreshment rooms were built in the angle between. Sir Matthew Digby Wyatt designed the station frontage and interiors of the new Temple Meads in a French Gothic style.

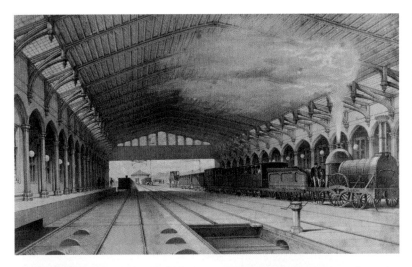

Left This illustration of the newly opened Temple Meads terminus evokes something of its grandeur and loftiness. The mock hammer-beam roof, with its central span of 74ft, was pierced along the length of its sides by skylights and ventilating funnels. The centre of the shed was occupied by five tracks. The arrival and departure platforms were 19ft deep and covered by arcades of neo-Tudor arches. On the right can be seen the 2-2-2 steam locomotive *Arrow*, of a type used extensively on the GWR in its formative years. *Author's collection*

Left The original Temple Meads goods shed in a lithograph by J. C. Bourne, 1846. *Author's collection*

What's left today?

Redundant as the main GWR terminus station after 1868, the old Temple Meads station was lucky to escape the developers after the shed was permanently closed to rail traffic almost a century later on 6 September 1966; it could so easily have been torn down to build yet more office blocks for the city. The neo-Tudor façade remains virtually intact except for the right-hand wing and portal, which was removed in 1878 to allow construction of ramp access to the new station.

The old station building, with its offices and trainshed, was rescued by the Empire and Commonwealth Trust in the early

Right Brunel's original terminus was extended during the 1870s, the length of the platforms being almost doubled. This was the sorry state of the building in the mid-1990s, when it was being used as a car park. In the background can be seen the furthermost end of the original 220ft-long trainshed. *Author*

Below An enlarged Temple Meads station was built in 1878. Today's station is not a terminus but offers passengers through services to destinations nationwide, including London. *Author*

1980s with the active support of the Railway Heritage Trust, English Heritage and the guidance of the Brunel Engineering Centre Trust. Its significance was recognised by listing it as Grade I and nomination for World Heritage Site status. Today it is used for office accommodation.

The trainshed is now known as the Engine Shed and is used as a conference centre, the enlarged Francis Fox/Digby Wyatt building of 1878 acting as the busy main-line Temple Meads station.

Rail tunnels and viaducts

Box Tunnel, Wiltshire

Completing the final section of the GWR, from Chippenham to Bath, in the late 1830s presented Brunel with the most physically difficult and technically challenging problems of the entire venture. His tendency to choose dramatic solutions to engineering problems perhaps partly explains his decision to dig a tunnel almost two miles long beneath Box Hill, in preference to a cutting.

Sceptics had forecast terrible calamities for the tunnel if work went ahead, describing the scheme as 'monstrous, extraordinary, most dangerous and impracticable'. Because of the planned falling gradient of 1 in 100 from one end of the tunnel to the other, the detractors argued that if a train's brakes failed at the higher end of the tunnel it would career through the darkness, accelerating all the time, and emerge at the other end travelling at a speed of 120mph, which would suffocate the passengers.

Nevertheless, work had begun on the tunnel in September 1836 under the watchful eyes of Brunel and his resident engineer William Glennie, when six permanent and two temporary shafts were sunk into the top of Box Hill down to rail level by the contractors, Paxton and Orton. Each shaft measured about 25ft in diameter and varied in depth from 125ft to 293ft, their

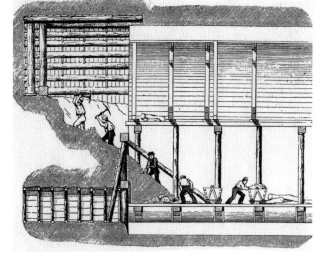

Above The most likely tunnelling method employed in the construction of Box Tunnel. *Author's collection*

purpose being to ventilate the fume-filled tunnel and to remove spoil from the workings. The shafts were completed in the autumn of 1837 and the digging of the first 880yd of tunnel from the Corsham end was commenced by the contractors, Lewis and Brewer. The remaining distance of some 2,300yd was contracted in February 1838 to George Burge of Herne Bay, who agreed to complete the job in 30 months.

The tunnelling was an extremely arduous process with some 1,200 navvies blasting and digging their way through solid stone and clay, whilst a team of 100 horses dragged away the tons of spoil, which finally totalled some 247,000cu yd. The work consumed huge quantities of materials: take, for example, the ton each of gunpowder and of candles which were consumed each week during the tunnel's protracted five-year construction. Steam pumps struggled to keep the workings free of water which on many occasions filled the tunnel through fissures in the rock and threatened to hold up work indefinitely.

Delays caused by flooding, quicksand and super-hard rock slowed excavations to such a snail's pace that Burge found himself unable to make progress at the rate laid down in his contract. As a result of this he crossed swords with Brunel and Glennie, Brunel refusing to pay Burge the full sum due to him until work was speeded up.

Carving a tunnel through almost two miles of rock and clay in such primitive working conditions claimed the lives of some 100 navvies over the course of the five years in which it was built. In the months of frantic activity leading to its completion Brunel was compelled to pay bonuses to ensure speedy work from the foremen and navvies, and it is believed that in the closing months up to 4,000 navvies and 300 horses were employed to finish digging Box Tunnel. The work was eventually completed in the spring of 1841, when the tunnellers broke through the rock into daylight.

When finally opened in June 1841 the tunnel was the longest in Great Britain, at 9,636ft. Lined almost completely with bricks, some 30 million of which were used during its construction, the

Right Six miles west of Chippenham the railway plunges into the 3,212yd Box Tunnel. This J. C. Bourne lithograph depicting of the western portal in 1846, only a few years after its completion, shows well the classical treatment of its façade. To the left of the tunnel mouth is an example of the disc-and-crossbar signal, designed by Brunel. *Author's collection*

tunnel was excavated on a gradient of 1 in 100 falling westwards through Box Hill towards Bath. Its arched portals are finished in Bath stone to a classical style topped by a balustrade.

What's left today?

Box Tunnel is in constant use every day by passenger and freight trains travelling the line between London and Bristol. So too are all of the tunnels listed below.

Other Brunel tunnels in the West Country

Between Box and Bristol:

Middle Hill Tunnel, Box, Wiltshire (594ft).

Sydney Gardens East Tunnel, Bath (231ft).

Sydney Gardens West Tunnel (297ft).

Twerton Short Tunnel, Twerton, Bath (135ft).

Twerton Long Tunnel (792ft).

Saltford Tunnel (528ft).

St Anne's Park No 3 Tunnel, Bristol (3,050ft).

St Anne's Park No 2 Tunnel (462ft).

Elsewhere:

Sapperton Tunnel, Gloucestershire.

Mickleton Tunnel, Chipping Campden, Gloucestershire.

Whitehall Tunnel, Somerset/Devon.

Below The façades of Box Tunnel's two portals have altered little over the years, as can be seen from this picture of an HST exiting the western portal. Today's rail traveller can pass through the tunnel at speeds of up to 125mph without the dangers of asphyxiation feared by some observers in the 1840s. *Author*

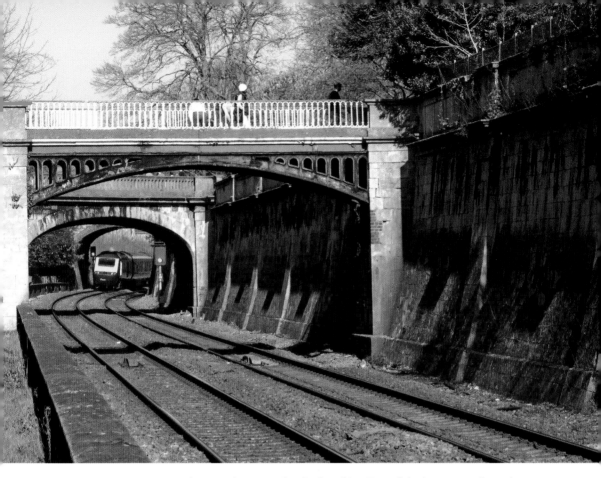

Above Within a couple of miles of Box Tunnel the line passes through Sydney Gardens, on the eastern edge of Bath. In order to accommodate Brunel's proposed route for the GWR the Kennet & Avon Canal was diverted here, and a massive retaining wall built to keep the canal where it was. *Author*

Right A contemporary Bourne lithograph depicting the view west, complete with retaining wall for the canal and a cluster of attractive Brunel-designed over-bridges in stone, and iron and timber. The navvies would have been working next to the signal light on the down (right-hand) track in the previous photograph.
Author's collection

Left After rumbling through Sydney Gardens' East and West tunnels trains emerge into daylight onto the curved 255yd-long Dolemeads Viaduct before again crossing the Avon. In this view, recorded from the tree-crowned heights of Beechen Cliff, the western portal of Sydney Gardens West Tunnel can be seen top left, St James' Bridge being in the foreground. *Author*

Above Saltford Tunnel, with Brunel's Tunnel House in the background. *Jon Godfrey*

Left St James' Bridge as it is today, viewed from the river walk leading to Widcombe. Much patching of the original stonework with engineers' brick is evident. *Author*

4 TRANSATLANTIC SEA TRAVEL

PS Great Western

Designed to carry passengers swiftly and comfortably between England and North America, the *Great Western* effectively extended the GWR's terminus from Bristol to New York. Her copper-sheathed wooden hull was built using traditional methods but with extra longitudinal stiffening incorporated into the design, to withstand the heaviest of Atlantic seas.

Powered by a pair of side-lever-type steam engines driving two paddle wheels, the *Great Western* was the largest vessel yet built. Below decks her passengers could relax in the sumptuous surroundings of her 75ft-long saloon.

Inevitably, great kudos attached to being the first company to operate a transatlantic steam-paddle-wheeler service, and this stirred the competitive instincts of a number of other steam-navigation companies at England's other two major ports, Liverpool and London. Each port laid down its own vessel in a bid to beat the *Great Western*, respectively the *Liverpool* and the *British Queen*. When it became evident that Brunel's ship was going to be launched and in revenue service long before those of the opposition the London-based British & American Steam

Above The *Great Western* at her moorings at Broad Pill, downstream on the River Avon.

Navigation Co cheated by substituting a small paddle-wheeler, the *Sirius*, for its not-yet-completed *British Queen*. This, combined with an ill-timed engine-room fire aboard the *Great Western*, conspired to put Brunel's ship behind the *Sirius* in the dash across the North Atlantic in April 1838.

Although the *Sirius* was first to arrive in New York on 23 April after 19 days at sea and ahead of the *Great Western*, she did so having been pushed almost beyond her design limits by her captain and arrived with dangerously low reserves of coal on board. When the *Great Western* arrived a matter of hours after the *Sirius*, having spent just 15 days at sea, she did so in style, with a faster crossing time and with ample reserves of coal in her bunkers. The *Sirius* won the race inasmuch as she was the first to reach New York, but Brunel's *Great Western* established that steam navigation was safe and practicable, setting a standard to which operators of transatlantic passenger vessels would henceforward have to aspire.

Over the following eight years the *Great Western* plied the waters of the North Atlantic, making 67 crossings, one eastbound journey taking just 12 days and six hours. However, her great size caused difficulties in navigating the river approaches to Bristol City Docks, so she worked from a deep-water anchorage at Kingroad, in the Bristol Channel. For several years passengers and cargo were ferried to and from her by Bristol tugs and barges, but in 1843 the *Great Western* was moved to Liverpool's Coburg Dock, from where she was operated with less expense to her owners. In 1845, in an unsolicited testimonial to the high quality of Brunel's construction techniques and materials, a Lloyd's surveyor declared the *Great Western* to be 'as sound in material and as perfect in form as on the day she was launched'. Her career finally came to an end in October 1856, when she and another ship were sold by her then owner, the West India Royal Mail Steam Packet Co, to a breaker at Vauxhall, on the River Thames, for £11,500 the pair.

Below An ancestor of the author sailed on the *Great Western* to join his regiment in North America in 1839. This is the entry from a contemporary family journal recording the occasion. *Author*

PS *Great Western*

Launched	19 July 1837
Length overall	236ft
Breadth of hull	35ft 4in
Draught	16ft 8in
Gross registered tonnage	1,320 tons
Displacement	2,300 tons
Hull material	Wood
Machinery	Two 450hp side-lever direct-acting steam engines driving two cycloidal paddle wheels, each of 28ft 9in diameter
Maximum speed	12kt
Capacity	260 cabins, 148 passengers
Cargo capacity	200 tons
Builder	William Patterson, Bristol (1836/7)
Fate	Scrapped at Greenwich (1857)

What's left today?

Sadly, nothing now remains of the *Great Western*. A plaque commemorating the ship's launch on 19 July 1837 can be seen 15ft up on the wall at the end of the Prince's Wharf buildings (Wapping Road end). The dock in which the ship was built has now been in-filled and is beneath M Shed, the Museum of Bristol.

Above A plaque high on the outside wall of the M Shed Bristol Museum commemorates the launch of the PS *Great Western* near this spot in July 1837. *Author*

Right Built 1837–9, the Royal Western Hotel in Great George Street, Bristol, was designed by R.S. Pope in collaboration with Brunel. The hotel was an important link in Brunel's concept of a through link from London to New York via Bristol. Passengers who had travelled down from London to Bristol on the GWR stayed at the hotel overnight before embarking for New York on the *Great Western*. Today only the façade remains, the building behind being used as offices by Bristol City Council. *Author*

SS Great Britain

When the sorry-looking hulk of the SS *Great Britain* was towed sedately up the River Avon to Bristol on 5 July 1970, following her epic 7,000-mile ocean voyage from the Falkland Islands, she was returning home for the first time since her launch from the same dock 127 years before.

When launched from the Great Western Dock on 19 July 1843 the *Great Britain* represented the very latest in ship design. She was the first ship built of iron and driven by a screw propeller to cross the watery wastes of the North Atlantic to America, setting new standards in engineering, reliability, speed and luxury. The *Great Britain* also represented a major challenge to America's dominance of the passenger trade in these waters, with its fast sailing packets.

Originally conceived by Brunel as a large, wooden-hulled paddle-wheeler along similar lines to his earlier *Great Western,* the *Great Britain* was initially known as the *City of New York*. However, the great engineer was so influenced by the iron-hulled design of a small paddle-wheeler named *Rainbow* which visited Bristol in 1838 that he decided his new ship, too, must be made of iron. Ten months after the first keel plates were laid down on 19 July 1839, further changes to his plans resulted from a demonstration of screw propulsion given at Bristol by another small vessel, the *Archimedes*. Consequently, work was suspended on the vessel's paddle engines

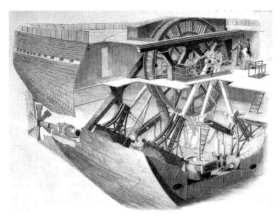

Above A contemporary cutaway drawing showing the steam engine installed in the *Great Britain*.
The Illustrated London News

and her means of propulsion was changed from a pair of side-mounted paddle wheels to a single stern-mounted screw. Her name was also changed at this stage to *Great Britain*.

The methods employed by Brunel in the construction of the *Great Britain's* iron hull were revolutionary for her day and represented a significant but necessary departure from timber shipbuilding practice. Brunel's design showed a greater concern for longitudinal strength than was hitherto the case and he achieved this by fitting a series of 10 iron girders running the length of the ship's bottom, on top of which he attached iron decking, in effect creating a double bottom – a feature of ship construction today. Five transverse bulkheads divided the ship into six watertight compartments, and two longitudinal bulkheads divided the ship up to main deck level. The large central section thus formed was occupied by the huge engines and boilers while the side compartments were used as coal bunkers.

A 1,600hp four-cylinder coal-fired steam engine was used to drive a single six-bladed 15ft 6in-diameter propeller, aft of which was fitted a balanced rudder, which gave the *Great Britain* a light and sensitive helm. Six masts were also fitted to enable her to take advantage of favourable winds thus enabling her to save valuable coal. Five masts fitted with fore and aft sails were hinged at their bases on the weather deck, while the main mast was made of

Right A recent view along the promenade deck inside the restored *Great Britain*. *Author*

iron, square-rigged and stepped right down through the decks to the keel. A 38ft funnel was fitted amidships. Eighteen skylights on the weather (top) deck gave light to the promenade deck below, while the engine-room roof included a huge skylight through which passengers could observe the workings of the impressive machinery within.

The *Great Britain* was floated from her dry dock on 19 July 1843 in the presence of Prince Albert the Prince Consort and a huge crowd of excited onlookers, who lined the quaysides and surrounding hills. Fitting out followed her launch, and it was not until late in 1844 that she was ready to commence her sea trials. Before she could emerge from the Cumberland Basin into the River Avon emergency widening of the two locks had to be undertaken, the vessel having become wedged between the coping stones on either side. These were quickly removed and the great ship finally emerged into the river.

The *Great Britain's* trial voyage around Land's End and up the English Channel to the Thames began on 23 January 1845, under the command of Captain James Hosken. *The Illustrated London News* of 1 February carried the following glowing testimonial to her fine design and construction and to the company that built her.

'On board the *Great Britain* Steam-ship, River Thames, Jan 26, 1845.

"We, the undersigned passengers on board the Great Britain steam-ship, on her experimental voyage from Bristol to London, having witnessed her performances during a stiff gale and a heavy sea, and amidst generally unfavourable weather, feel called upon to express our conviction of her great length being no detriment to her excellent sailing qualities and her sea-worthiness …

"We further beg to express our high sense of the spirited conduct of the company by whom so great a monument of commercial enterprise was designed and carried out; and to congratulate them, and the engineers, and artisans employed in her construction, upon the success which has attended their labours, as evinced by the results of a voyage so well calculated to test her powers as the present has been."'

The ship's maiden voyage, from Liverpool to New York, was made six months later, on 26 July, with a small complement of 50 passengers, the crossing taking just 14 days and 21 hours – half

the time taken by the fastest sailing packets of the day. But on her fifth transatlantic voyage, with 180 passengers on board, disaster struck on the night of 22 September 1846, when, due to a navigational error, she ran aground on the beach of Dundrum Bay, Co Down, Ireland. It was not until 27 August 1847 that she was finally refloated and towed to Liverpool for repairs.

Because the SS *Great Britain* had been underinsured by her owner, the Great Western Steamship Co, the cost of her salvage proved prohibitive, and the company was forced to sell her, along with the *Great Western*. Bought by Gibbs, Bright & Co, the *Great Britain* was re-engined, while her were masts reduced to four, and structural alterations were made to enable her to carry up to 730 passengers.

A successful trial voyage to New York was made in 1852, and, later that year, on 21 August, the *Great Britain* sailed for Australia with 630 passengers on board, the first of many such voyages made over the next 20 years.

In 1876 the *Great Britain* was laid up at Birkenhead, and in 1882 she was bought by Antony Gibbs, Sons & Co for use as a cargo sailing ship. She was stripped of all her passenger accommodation, her engines were removed, and her hull was clad with pitch pine above the waterline. She made a number of voyages to San Francisco and Panama, carrying coal from South Wales, until she got into difficulties in bad weather rounding Cape Horn in April 1886. Leaking badly, her cargo having shifted, she developed a serious list to port, and her fore and main topgallant masts were lost overboard, prompting her captain to seek shelter at Port Stanley, in the Falkland Islands. The cost of repairs once again proved to be her undoing, and, having been offered for sale, she was bought by the Falkland Islands Co, for use as a store ship for coal and wool.

By 1937 the *Great Britain* had finally outlived her usefulness, and she was towed out of the harbour at Port Stanley and beached at Sparrow Cove. Holes were knocked in her stern (and one amidships) to ensure that she would not float off, and she was left to rot. But this was not the end for Brunel's great iron-hulled wonder.

Below Water is pumped out of the flooded interior of the *Great Britain*'s hull in preparation for a pontoon to be sunk under her then pumped out to make her float. *South American Pictures / Marion Morrison*

Above The sorry-looking hulk of the *Great Britain* in Sparrow Cove, Falkland Islands, in 1969. *South American Pictures/Marion Morrison*

Below The *Great Britain* passes beneath Brunel's Clifton Suspension Bridge on her return to her birthplace. *South American Pictures/Marion Morrison*

In the 1950s interest in salvaging the *Great Britain* was shown in the United States and at home in England, but it was not until 1968 that a naval architect travelled all the way from England to Sparrow Cove to assess the viability of refloating her. With financial and technical problems finally overcome, the *Great Britain* was refloated, and a pontoon, the *Mulus III*, submerged beneath her hull. The pontoon was then pumped out, lifting the ship out of the water. She was firmly secured atop the *Mulus III*, and the first stage of the 7,000-mile voyage home began on 24 April 1970, via Port Stanley and Montevideo, towed by the salvage tug *Varius II*. The longest leg of the *Great Britain*'s homeward journey began on 6 May, and on 22 June the ship and pontoon arrived off the Welsh coast, where Bristol tug boats took over for the short journey to Avonmouth Docks. The *Great Britain* arrived to a tumultuous welcome, and over the next few days arrangements were made to take her off the pontoon in Avonmouth graving dock. Afloat on her own bottom, she was towed up the River Avon on 5 July, watched by thousands of spectators, and tied up for two weeks at Y Wharf in the city docks, awaiting a spring tide high enough to ease her through the shallow entrance to the Great Western Dry Dock. By coincidence this fell on 19 July, exactly 127 years after her launch in 1843.

SS *Great Britain*

Launched	19 July 1843
Length overall	322ft
Breadth of hull	50ft 6in
Draught	16ft
Gross registered tonnage	3,270 tons
Displacement	3,618 tons
Hull material	Iron
Machinery	One 1,000hp V-cranked overhead direct-acting steam engine driving one 15ft 6in-diameter six-bladed screw
Maximum speed	12kt
Capacity	26 single cabins, 113 two-berth cabins, 252 passengers
Cargo capacity	1,200 tons
Builder	William Patterson, Bristol (1839-43)
Fate	Preserved at Great Western Dock, Bristol

Right The *Great Britain* was the first large ship to be equipped with a clipper bow, designed for speed. In this stem-on view the bow displays its fine lines; above the waterline her hull bulges in order to provide as much space as possible on board. *Author*

Below To prevent further corrosion of the *Great Britain*'s iron hull a climate-controlled dehumidification chamber has been created by roofing the Great Western Dry Dock with an airtight and watertight glass 'sea'. *Author*

Right An authentic replica of the 1,000hp marine steam engine gives an idea of the great power at the heart of the *Great Britain*.
Author

What's left today?

Today the *Great Britain* has been transformed into one of the UK's most innovative museum and visitor attractions, and in 2013 she welcomed more than 170,000 visitors.

Returning *Great Britain* to her Bristol home in 1970 was just the start of an even longer journey of conservation and preservation. Since then Brunel's ship has been subject to an extensive and ongoing restoration programme, the cost of which has been underwritten largely by the generosity of a number of individuals – in particular the philanthropists Sir Jack Hayward and John Paul Getty Jr – as well as donations and gifts in kind from corporate benefactors. In 1995 the organisers of the SS *Great Britain* project submitted a bid for Heritage Lottery funding, but without success. Undeterred, they lodged a new application and in 2002 were successful in securing £10 million towards the ship's restoration.

The major areas for conservation have been the ship's weather deck and her iron hull. The weather deck has been replaced with a steel deck clad in Jarrah hardwood for realism, with an air-circulation space of 1¼in between the two layers to preserve both surfaces from moisture damage. However, the most fragile part of the ship is below the waterline where it was exposed to salty seawater for over 127 years. Research has shown that the iron hull can survive if it is protected from humidity in a very dry environment. The solution has been to enclose the *Great Britain* below the waterline inside a climate-controlled dehumidification chamber, made by roofing over with glass the dry dock in which she sits. The glass 'sea' overhead provides an airtight and watertight environment as well as a novel way of displaying the ship. Two giant dehumidification machines filter the air inside the dock to reduce relative humidity to a manageable 20%, effectively halting the corrosion process.

Above deck the ship has been re-masted and re-rigged, while internally the passenger spaces have been fully restored to recreate the ship as it would have been on a voyage to Australia, complete with sounds and smells, a galley, stores, passenger and crew cabins, bathrooms, staterooms and a giant cargo hold. An impressive 100-ton replica marine steam engine was built at a cost of £400,000 with significant support from Rolls-Royce. Although driven by electricity, its pistons and flywheel give a powerful impression of how the original engine would have looked and felt. It is a truly awe-inspiring piece of machinery to watch in motion.

Below Plan drawings of the PSS *Great Eastern* *(see overleaf). US Library of Congress*

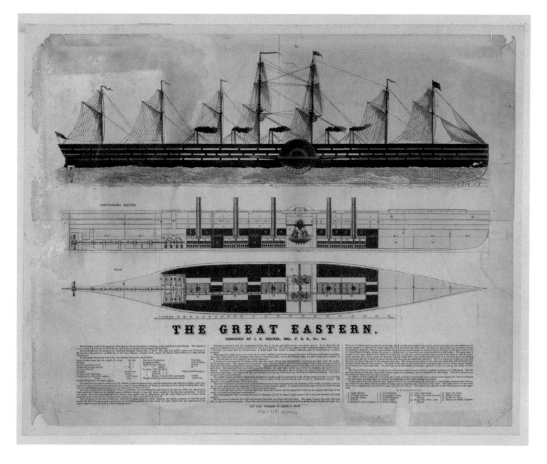

THE GREAT EASTERN.

PSS Great Eastern

Brunel's third and last great shipbuilding project was the construction of a huge steamship capable of sailing around the world non-stop without refuelling. Sadly, the problems of finance, personality clashes with his partner and builder of the ship, John Scott Russell, and the latter's eventual repudiation of the contract placed a fatal strain on Brunel's already failing health.

The contract for the construction of the enormous vessel – 10 times the displacement and more than twice the length of the *Great Britain* – was signed in 1853, and work began alongside the River Thames at Scott Russell's yard at Millwall, on the Isle of Dogs. Unlike Brunel's other ships, the *Leviathan*, as she was known initially, was to be built in a yard and launched sideways down a shallow slipway and into the Thames.

Brunel should perhaps have been more wary of the outcome when Scott Russell tendered £377,200 for building the *Leviathan*, against Brunel's estimate of £500,000. However, Scott Russell was regarded as the greatest marine engineer of his day, and in any case Brunel was too busy with other projects to go through Scott Russell's costings with a fine toothcomb. This seems a little strange, given the care he exercised when checking the expense claims made by his assistants and engineers, querying the slightest inconsistency in their figure work. Perhaps it was a case of being penny-wise, pound-foolish.

Below John Scott Russell, builder of the *Great Eastern*, with whom Brunel fell out early on in the construction of the ship.

Below right Brunel's *Great Eastern* was a huge steamship in every sense of the word; her massive hull alone was built of 30,000 iron plates, each held in its place by 100 rivets. This engraving shows work underway on the construction of the ship's central compartment at John Scott Russell's yard in Millwall during 1857. *The Illustrated London News*

Left The Isle of Dogs, Millwall and Greenwich Reach, site of the construction and launch of the *Great Eastern*.
Ian Black

Below Earnest faces watch intently as attempts are made to launch the *Great Eastern* in November 1857. From left to right are Captain William Harrison, late of the Cunard Line, Brunel's chief assistant William Jacomb, Brunel himself and Thomas Treadwell, railway contractor of London and Gloucester, to whom the contract for the launching ways and cradles was let.

During the great ship's protracted construction relations between the two men became progressively more sour, Scott Russell withholding progress and technical reports. When Scott Russell announced in 1855 that the bank had withdrawn his credit facilities Brunel was forced to sink much of his own capital into financing the building programme. Eventually, having paid £292,295 to Scott Russell (who had completed little more than a quarter of the hull), Brunel took over the management himself.

The launch was planned for 3 November 1857, but the problems of sliding a load of some 12,000 tons for 250ft initially proved insuperable. Eventually, with the aid of powerful hydraulic rams, the *Great Eastern*, as she was now called, slid into the River Thames on 31 January 1858.

With the arduous work involved in preparing his great ship for launching Brunel became very sick, and his doctor ordered that he spend the winter in a warm climate. Upon his return from Egypt in May 1859 Brunel discovered to his great anger that in his absence the directors of the company formed to fit out the *Great Eastern* had appointed Scott Russell to the task. Brunel then took immediate charge of the ship to prepare her for her sea trials but suffered a stroke four days before she sailed for Weymouth.

The *Great Eastern* began her sea trials on 9 September but suffered an explosion in the waterjacket surrounding the base of

the forward funnel, the blast blowing the funnel into the air and killing six crewmen. By a stroke of luck none of the passengers was hurt. Meanwhile, at his home in Duke Street, London, Brunel lay paralysed in his bed but was eager for news of the sea trials. Perhaps the ill tidings he received hastened his end, for he died six days later.

Right Measuring 695ft overall and 120ft in the beam over the paddle boxes, the *Great Eastern* was an enormous vessel. *US Library of Congress*

Below Scott Russell's paddle engines for the *Great Eastern* were commensurately huge – four cylinders, each 6ft 2in in diameter with a stroke of 14ft and a nominal output of 1,000hp. *Author's collection*

As for the *Great Eastern,* she made several passenger voyages across the North Atlantic, but the excessive cost of rectifying recurring mechanical problems forced her owners to sell her in 1862. Her great size appealed to the Telegraph Construction Co, which bought her and used her for laying undersea telegraphic cables. The passenger accommodation was removed to enable huge iron drums to be installed, each containing thousands of miles of cable. Perhaps the greatest failing of the ship was that she was underpowered for her size; contemporary marine engines were simply not powerful or reliable enough. Another factor which militated against her was that she arrived on the scene a little before any worthwhile economic function existed for her to perform. She ended her days as a showboat on the River Mersey, finally being broken up in 1889.

PSS *Great Eastern*

Launched	31 January 1858
Length overall	692ft
Breadth of hull	82.7ft
Over paddle boxes	118ft
Draught	30ft
Gross registered tonnage	18,915 tons
Displacement	(25ft draught) 22,000 tons
Displacement	(30ft draught) 27,419 tons
Hull material	Iron
Machinery	One 1,000hp four-cylinder oscillating steam engine driving two 56ft-diameter paddle wheels; one 1,600hp four-cylinder horizontal direct-acting steam engine driving one 24ft-diameter four-bladed screw propeller
Maximum speed	13.5kt
Capacity	596 (cabin), 2,400 (steerage)
Builder	J. Scott Russell, Millwall, London (1854–9)
Fate	Scrapped at New Ferry, Birkenhead (1889–91)

It was not until 47 years later that the first ship to exceed the tonnage of the *Great Eastern* was built – the *Lusitania.*

What's left today?

As is the case with the *Great Western,* sadly nothing now remains of the *Great Eastern,* but at low tide the slipways used for launching her can just be made out in the river mud *(see page 145)*.

5 DOCK SCHEMES

Bristol – South Entrance Lock and swivel bridge (1845–9)

During the 1830s the Bristol Docks Co realised there was a growing need for a broader entrance lock from the tidal River Avon into the non-tidal Floating Harbour.

Since the construction of the latter, in the early 19th century by William Jessop, few improvements of any significance had been made to the city's port facilities. The city fathers and the docks company appreciated that substantial improvements were necessary not only to arrest the dock's relative decline compared with the other major ports, like London and Liverpool, but also to improve facilities for the new breed of large steamships for which Brunel himself was principally responsible. Indeed it would later prove to Brunel's advantage to improve facilities, after his *Great Britain* became wedged in the narrow entrance to the old lock in 1844.

Brunel had so impressed the Society of Merchant Venturers with his design for the Clifton Bridge in 1831 that the following year its members introduced him to the Bristol Docks Co, which invited him to make a report on the problems afflicting the docks. These arose primarily from silting, and Brunel's report of August 1832 recommended several ways of improving matters. However, not all

Above The view *c*1906. Brunel's original iron swivel bridge over the South Entrance Lock has now been moved but can still be seen a few yards away on the lock side adjacent to the North Entrance Lock.
Author's collection

Left Brunel's rebuilt South Entrance Lock can be seen on the right of this picture, and next to it the old North Lock, which was closed permanently in 1873. The profiled walls and floor of Brunel's lock can be appreciated in this view. In the late 1860s the houses on the left were demolished to make way for a new North Entrance Lock (designed by T. Howard), which is still in use today.
Bristol Museum

of his ideas were instantly seized upon, although over the following 15 years he was commissioned by the company commissioned to undertake specific improvements, among them raising the height of the Netham Weir to direct more water through the harbour and the construction of four culverts beneath the Overfall Dam at the western end of the Floating Harbour; three of these were to control the level of the water in the Float, while the fourth was to scour large quantities of silt into the Cut. As a result of this the Overfall Dam soon became known as the Underfall Dam.

Brunel had warned in 1835 that the small 33ft-wide South Lock needed to be rebuilt, but the docks company procrastinated over the issue, and it was not until 1844 that he was again invited to report on the condition of the South Lock. His estimate of £22,000 for a completely new lock measuring 54ft wide and 245ft long shocked the docks company, which was at that time experiencing severe financial hardship. Nevertheless, the need was pressing, and in 1845 Brunel was authorised to proceed without delay. However, the brisk pace of work did not last for long, thanks to a number of problems encountered during the course of construction, and the new lock was not ready for use until April 1849. The wrought-iron tubular swivel bridge over the lock – Brunel's first large wrought-iron opening bridge – was not completed until later that year.

Below Contemporary view showing the Overfall Dam (middle foreground) and beyond it the Cumberland Basin.
Bristol Museum

Right The South Entrance Lock today, sealed off by a concrete barrier and sluices from the Cumberland Basin.
Author

The completed South Entrance Lock measured 262ft long by 52ft wide at the entrance. Its carefully profiled elliptical walls and floor allowed maximum clearance for heavily laden vessels with a greater draught than was previously possible, together with maximum operating space for them once within the lock chamber itself. A novel feature of the lock was its single-leaf partially buoyant caisson gates, which were hinged and ran on cast-iron rails. The gates were swung by a manually operated capstan.

Brunel's South Entrance Lock served the Port of Bristol well until rendered obsolete by the opening of a new and larger entrance lock in 1879.

What's left today?

The South Entrance Lock survives to this day, although the single-leaf gates were removed in 1906, and the lock itself was sealed off. It is best viewed at low tide. The manually operated capstan also survives, along with the channels gouged in the stonework by its heavy chains. The iron swivel bridge designed by Brunel to carry traffic over the lock is now redundant, having been decommissioned in 1968, but remains *in situ* alongside the North Entrance Lock, in the shadow of its large modern equivalent, the Plimsoll Bridge. David Neale, former Bristol City Docks Engineer, can be thanked for highlighting the historical significance of Brunel's swivel bridge, having effectively saved it from the scrapman's blow-torch.

Left Brunel's swivel bridge is the oldest surviving example of the engineer's wrought-iron tubular-girder construction. Beyond can be seen the electrically operated Plimsoll Bridge. *Author*

Below The mechanism for turning the swivel bridge is still in place and is potentially still in working order. *Author*

At the time of writing (2014) the bridge is Bristol's only abandoned Brunel structure. It is Grade II* Listed and, sadly, is on the English Heritage 'At Risk' register. However, the future looks healthier now that the bridge is undergoing refurbishment by the Brunel Swivel Bridge Group. The project, co-ordinated by Maggie Shapland and led by Geoff Wallis, of Dorothea Restorations, is supported by several local societies, including the Clifton & Hotwells Improvement Society and Bristol Industrial Archaeological Society. Its aims are to improve the dockside site's neglected appearance, to slow the deterioration of the bridge structure, to raise awareness of its historical significance and to progress the refurbishment of some of its working parts.

Brunel's swivel bridge at the Cumberland Basin was his first large wrought-iron opening bridge. The structure rotates on four fixed wheels in contact with a solid ring underneath the bridge, turned by an hydraulic mechanism of twin rams located in pits. These are connected to the turning ring under the bridge via a substantial wire cable. Before being converted to hydraulic operation the turning mechanism was a hand-turned crank, similar to that used on old train turntables. The pistons and chains are still in place today.

Monkwearmouth Dock, Sunderland (1835–7)

With the increase in maritime trade during the 1820s the need became apparent for the construction of new docks at Sunderland to enable the river port to compete effectively with docks further south on the Durham coast It was in November 1831 that Brunel made the long journey north to Monkwearmouth in order to meet local merchants and businessmen with a view to securing his appointment as engineer to the new docks scheme. Despite the frustration of having his initial plans for the docks rejected by Parliament the following year, he submitted a revised plan, which was approved, and work began in 1835.

The North Dock, as it was known, was designed by Brunel and built by him between 1835 and 1837, with Michael Lane as resident engineer. It was opened in 1837 by the Wearmouth Dock Co but in 1846 was bought out by George Hudson's York, Newcastle & Berwick Railway. A suspension bridge designed by Brunel to span the River Wear to bring coal from the south side of the river was never built.

Due to its modest size and poor position on the River Wear the dock was never a great success; at no time between 1838 and 1858 did the coal exported through the dock exceed 8.3% of the total exports from Sunderland, and it would soon be completely overshadowed by Sunderland's South Docks, which opened in 1850.

Right An aerial view of Monkwearmouth (North) Dock c1950; clearly visible is the timber traffic which was the dock's primary workload from the late 19th century. The photograph predates the 1953 scheme for the in-filling of the eastern half of the dock to provide a quay for the adjacent ship-repair yard. *Tyne & Wear Museum Service*

By the late 19th century the North Dock was used for timber traffic by its owner, the North Eastern Railway, and Armstrong Addison, which produced many of the NER's sleepers and timber bridge baulks. Over the ensuing years it declined in fortune, being used only for the occasional shipment of lime and as a mooring place for large privately owned yachts — a portent of things to come, perhaps. In 1953 the eastern side of the North Dock was filled in to provide a quay for vessels being repaired in a nearby yard. In the early 1980s facilities for roll-on, roll-off ships were constructed, bringing a short-lived new lease of life to Brunel's old dock, but industrial use of the North Dock ceased in the early 1990s.

What's left today?

In the 1990s a controversial redevelopment scheme by Tyne & Wear Development Corporation saw the North Dock converted into a boating marina, with housing along its quays and at North Sands. Today the resulting Sunderland Marina, with 88 fully serviced pontoon berths and facilities for Sunderland Yacht Club, can accommodate around 200 vessels; the Marine Activities Centre was opened in 1994 by round-the-world yachtsman Chay Blyth. The transformation of Brunel's North Dock forms part of St Peter's Riverside, a wider regeneration of derelict land along the banks of the River Wear, which project has successfully opened up Sunderland's long-neglected industrial landscape, closed to the public for more than a century, to create recreational and living

Left In the early 1980s the North Dock was provided with facilities to service Ro-Ro ships. This 1984 photograph illustrates the condition of the dock in its later years. Notice the weed-strewn railway tracks in the foreground (left) and the removal of the lock gates. *Tyne & Wear Museum Service*

space. Today, although most of its original walls and outline remain, the former North Dock bears very little resemblance to its once rough-and-ready existence as a coal and timber dock.

Briton Ferry Dock, Glamorgan (1851–61)

During the 1840s the industrialisation of South Wales quickened with the growth of heavy industry. In the Neath area an iron-smelting works was built beside the River Neath, to be quickly followed by two steelworks, five tinplate works and a galvanising works, along with their associated industries. Trade on the river therefore increased dramatically, with regular cargoes of copper and tin ores inwards and coal, limestone, culm, iron and various refined metals and manufactured goods outwards. However, the shipping companies, which had until now been engaged in transporting coal from riverside wharves, found the harbour facilities along the Neath completely inadequate for this new boom in trade.

In 1846 a company was formed to establish new docks at Briton Ferry, but a financial crisis saw to it that nothing further was done until 1851. Strong lobbying of Parliament by Viscount Villiers,

Chairman of the Vale of Neath Railway Co, and H.S. Coke, Neath's Town Clerk, led to the passing that same year of the Briton Ferry Dock Act, which sanctioned the construction of a floating dock at Briton Ferry. Isambard Brunel was engaged as designer and engineer, and work commenced in 1853. To ensure the commercial success of the dock Brunel was further engaged to plan and develop a railway to transport coal from mines at Glyncorrwg, in the Valleys, to Briton Ferry. This was the South Wales Mineral Railway, authorised by an Act of 1853, which linked Briton Ferry with Glyncorrwg via Tonmawr and Cymmer. Brunel was also engaged in the planning and engineering of the South Wales Railway and Vale of Neath Railway, both of which would directly link the proposed dock with collieries in the Vale of Neath.

As would be the case with several more of his designs, Brunel did not live to see the completion of the dock, and it fell to contractor William Ritson to complete the work, with the specialist machinery installed by Sir William Armstrong. The dock was officially opened on 22 August 1861, in a blaze of ceremony and in spite of the torrential rain which sadly put paid to any outdoor celebrations. Shortly after 2pm the formal opening and the first shipment of coal were marked by a salute from the guns of the

Below The South Wales town of Briton Ferry and its dock, photographed c1905. Today none of the depicted industry survives, and the northernmost portion of the dock (nearest the camera), now in-filled, is crossed by two bridges carrying roads — the A48 (built in 1955) and the M4 (1994).
Cliff Morgan

91

2nd Artillery (Briton Ferry) Volunteers and a volley from the muskets of the Glamorganshire Rifle Volunteers. Significantly, the first ship to be loaded at the new wharves was the barque *Mary Stenson*, which then transported its cargo of coal to Liverpool for loading onto Brunel's transatlantic liner *Great Eastern*.

In one of the many florid speeches made that day to celebrate the opening (and duly reported the following day in *The Cambrian*, the local newspaper) Mr H.H. Vivian MP commented: 'The eminent engineer who planned the docks has been removed from us, but his works remain and will still do so. I believe Mr Brunel to be the greatest engineer who ever lived – not excluding Stephenson, Lock and others. When the asperities of the times have passed away from their minds they will see that his works are the greatest engineering works ever conceived.'

As built the inner dock measured more than 1,600ft in length by 400ft across, with a depth over the sill, on ordinary spring tides, of 25ft. The combined inner (or floating) dock of 11 acres and the outer tidal basin of 7½ acres were nearly ½ mile long. The sides of the dock were not walled-up like those at Bristol but were sloped off and strengthened by a deposit of slag from the nearby copper works. The piers at the dock entrance were of solid stone and built to withstand tidal action, as there was no entrance lock. At 56ft in length and with a depth in the middle of 31ft 6in the gate itself was, at the time of its construction, the widest single-span dock gate in the world. Made by Messrs Finch & Heath, of Chepstow, and weighing 140 tons, the gate was a wrought-iron buoyant structure consisting of five vertical internal bulkheads and six decks and was supported on one hinge, without any additional support in the form of rollers. Brunel had decided on this solution because the influx of sand from the outer basin and coal slag dropped into the dock itself could easily render the use of rollers at the foot of the gate impracticable. Water was admitted to some of the bulkheads to render the gate buoyant.

Approached along a 50ft-wide channel (at the mouth of the River Neath) which formed a tidal basin almost as large as the Brunel Dock itself, the dock was served by two railway lines which ran parallel with the dock on either side. These lines were linked to four coal-drops worked by hydraulic machinery; two were combined hoists, the other two flat drops. There were also a number of hydraulically operated cranes for the unloading of coal and ballast from ships' holds.

Once in operation the dock built up a thriving trade in both coastal and export shipments, as demonstrated by the total of 2,635 vessels that entered the dock in the financial year 1871/2. However, its fortunes were soon to change, for in 1873 the dock was taken over by the Great Western Railway. Thereafter trade declined steadily, due primarily to the GWR's preference for the use and development of the docks at Port Talbot and Swansea. The dock continued to trade into the 1930s, but after World War 2 it was abandoned, being no longer profitable, the last ship leaving the dock in 1959. Soon the dock gates were removed for scrap and dredging ceased, and it was not long before the dock itself became heavily silted up by the thick river mud that was washed in.

Neath Borough Council purchased the dock in 1969 and proposed to fill it with hardcore prior to turning the area into an industrial estate, but due to financial difficulties these plans were shelved in 1974. The future of the dock again looked in doubt when in 1990 work began on the building of the M4 motorway viaduct across the dock and River Neath, and it was feared that much of Brunel's work would be destroyed.

Below All that remained in 1973 of the wrought-iron buoyant dock gate after its dismantling. *Cliff Morgan*

Bottom Once the dock gate had been removed (centre top in this picture) and dredging ceased the dock rapidly silted up. This is the dock in 2014. *McNab*

Right A photograph of the dock and steelworks taken in 1973, this being the view south. The steelworks have now been demolished, and the site cleared. The M4 motorway viaduct crosses the dock to the north – and left – of here, while the dock north of this point has been filled in. The area visible in this picture is basically all that remains of Brunel's Floating Dock. At centre left, beneath the first chimney, is the Brunel Tower, which now enjoys Listed status, in common with the dock walls and inner basin, quoins and dock gate.
Cliff Morgan

The fight to save Briton Ferry Dock

In 1989 West Glamorgan County Council considered filling the dock's inner basin with spoil from the M4 motorway construction, as a means of removing what, in some quarters, was looked upon as an eyesore. Local councillors were appalled by this solution to the problem, arguing that in many other areas of the country people were fighting for facilities like those offered by the dock and that, with sympathetic redevelopment, it could play a major recreational role in the future of Briton Ferry.

At a public meeting in 1990 the Briton Ferry Brunel Dock Group was formed by local people with the twin aims of preserving and developing the historic Brunel dock. As a result of the group's intensive lobbying of local MPs, West Glamorgan County Council, the Welsh Office, the Welsh Development Agency and Costain Civil Engineering (contractors for the M4 link) the dockside Brunel Tower, the dock gate and its surrounding walls were accorded Listed Building status. Costain gave assurances that care would be taken to preserve as much as possible of the old dock and that any environmental damage during the course of construction work would be kept to a minimum.

Thankfully the local authority understood the importance of the dock to the town of Briton Ferry and its environs, recognising that future plans would have to include a comprehensive clearing-up and landscaping of the area around the dock, as well as the creation of a marina-type development for the dock itself, with light industry and facilities for the town situated alongside, similar to London's Docklands.

Two decades on there is still much to be done, and money has yet to be found to regenerate the site. Around £70,000 has already been spent preserving the Brunel Tower, and there has been some landscaping with the aim of eventually creating a marina, but this is a drop in the ocean. Perhaps if Briton Ferry were on the banks of the River Thames in London and not in South Wales the money would have been found by now, and the docks transformed into a vibrant amenity for the community.

What's left today?

The outer basin, gate entrance and surrounding walls and half the inner basin have been saved from destruction thanks to the efforts of the Briton Ferry Brunel Dock Group. However, half of the inner basin has been filled in to facilitate construction of the M4 motorway bridge across the dock. A barrier was built across the entrance to the dock, cutting it off from the tidal waters of the River Neath, so it is now empty of water but still badly silted and overgrown with grass and reeds. The bottom section of the unique wrought-iron buoyant dock gate survived the cutter's torch and remains beneath the silt at the dock entrance. On the eastern bank can be seen the preserved Brunel Tower; built to house the hydraulic accumulator (designed by William Armstrong) which operated the dock gate and cranes, this has been restored by the Brunel Dock Trust.

Despite the hard work of the Dock Group, plans for the future redevelopment of Briton Ferry Dock are still very much in the balance. Apathy over what should be done with the dock and a failure to arouse the interest of potential developers are partly to blame.

Great Western Docks, Mill Bay, Plymouth (1853–6)

In 1853 Brunel was retained as consulting engineer on the construction of a wet dock and a graving dock in Mill Bay, a large inlet in Plymouth Sound near the entrance to the Hamoaze. He also advised on the construction of a pier to shelter the dock's entrance gates from the sea. When opened for use in 1856 the 13-acre wet dock had a quay wall 13,940ft long and was 22ft deep at ordinary spring tides, being 16ft deep at neap tides. The entrance was closed by a pair of wrought-iron buoyant

Above An aerial view of the Great Western Docks (Mill Bay) and Stonehouse, Plymouth, recorded shortly after World War 2.

gates, each 48ft long and weighing 75 tons. Large scouring culverts were situated behind the side walls of the entrance, a pair of cylindrical sluice valves being incorporated into the dock gates themselves, to regulate the volume of water in the dock. The entrance to the graving dock was 80ft wide and was closed by a pair of wrought-iron buoyant gates of the same dimensions and construction as those for the entrance to the wet dock. With an overall length of 380ft and a width of 92ft, its depth over the sill was 28ft.

Brunel had also advised on the construction in 1852 of a 300ft-long floating pier in Mill Bay, for the benefit of steam shipping. It was connected to the shore by a double-span iron bridge, each span 125ft across, supported on a timber pier. The pontoon itself was capable of storing 4,000 tons of coal.

What's left today?

The Great Western Docks are now known as Mill Bay Docks and are owned by Associated British Ports. The graving dock was in-filled in the early 1970s, and a car ferry terminal built on it, used today by Brittany Ferries for its cross-Channel services to France and Spain. The wet dock has been partially in-filled, and the whole dock is now tidal. The southeastern side of the dock between Mill Bay and Trinity Pier has been redeveloped as a marina and housing complex in Plymouth's largest construction project since the postwar rebuilding of the city following the devastation of the Blitz. Mixing new homes with commercial and retail and leisure space the objective has been to cement Plymouth's position as one of Europe's finest waterfront cities. The new 171-berth King Point Marina, in the inner dock basin, opened in September 2013 as the centre-piece of the transformation of Mill Bay into a waterfront quarter. There is a rolling programme of work to develop the remainder of the site in successive phases, and a further phase of new homes at East Quay is due for completion in late 2014.

Brentford Dock, Middlesex (1855–9)

Brentford Dock was built to facilitate the interchange of goods between river barges linking waterside warehouses (and the Port of London) with the railway network – the Great Western, Brentford & Thames Junction Railway and the GWR at Southall. The quay walls are constructed of composite brick and mass concrete, with horizontal arches between counterfort piers (*i.e.* the piers are not visibly expressed). At the dock entrance to the River Thames is a large single-leaf tidal gate.

What's left today?

Brentford Dock closed in 1964, the area being redeveloped for housing, but the dock basin has been retained. Still visible are parts of Brunel's quay walls, the tidal gate (of which a section of the original top beam has been preserved) and one of the original water-line girder bridges. The sole surviving former railway bridge (Augustus Way Bridge) now serves as a road bridge.

Neyland Pontoon Dock, Milford Haven, Pembrokeshire (1857)

When the Great Western Railway finally reached West Wales in 1853 Brunel decided on Neyland, near Milford Haven in Pembrokeshire, as the site for a rail terminus to act as a hub for onward travel to the United States. At that time Neyland was little more than a coastal village with a shipyard and a few hundred inhabitants, but Brunel's interest was attracted by the deep water offshore, which made it an ideal location for a port for steam packets sailing to and from Ireland. With the arrival of the South Wales Railway on 15 April 1856 Neyland became a boom town overnight and for a brief period was popularly known as 'the Swindon of West Wales'. To service the passenger and livestock trade with Ireland Brunel designed and built a large floating pontoon, launched in 1857, which allowed the Irish steam packets to berth at Neyland at any state of tide. The pontoon structure measured 154ft in length, and some 300 tons of iron and 600 tons of timber were used in its construction.

Below A section of original Brunel broad-gauge railway track is now used as a barrier at Neyland, Pembrokeshire.
Derek Webb

Neyland prospered for 50 years as the West Wales terminus for the GWR and became a major trading port for Ireland, Portugal and Brazil. Brunel's PSS *Great Eastern* paid several visits and was moored offshore through the winter of 1860/1 for essential maintenance. The Irish trade was lost in 1906 when it was transferred to Fishguard, and, after 108 years, rail services to Neyland finally ceased in 1964 when Dr Beeching's axe fell.

What's left today?

The giant pontoon is long gone, but traces of the old railway line can still be seen in the form of the Brunel Cycle Route between Brunel Quay and Rosemarket. Other reminders of Brunel are to be found in local street names, while railway tracks can still be seen buried in modern tarmac, and sections of broad-gauge track have been incorporated into the barrier facing the sea. Regrettably a fine statue of Brunel by local sculptor Robert Thomas, which had been erected on the quayside, was stolen not long after its unveiling in 1999.

6 THE 'ATMOSPHERIC CAPER'

In the boom years of 'railway mania' leading up to the completion of the GWR route from London to Bristol (1841) and the Bristol & Exeter Railway line (1844) a number of proposals were put forward to extend the railway further still into the South West of England.

In July 1844 the act sanctioning construction of the 52-mile South Devon Railway (SDR) from Exeter to Plymouth received Royal Assent, and the following month Brunel, as engineer to the railway company, presented the SDR's directors with a detailed report, in which he enthusiastically recommended an up-to-the-minute form of traction to overcome the anticipated operating difficulties on the railway.

The SDR's steep gradients and sharp winding curves posed something of a problem to the early generation of steam locomotives, which lacked sufficient reserves of power to cope. Brunel, ever mindful of his claim and belief that his railway should offer passengers a fast and comfortable ride, turned his attention to another form of traction, known as the 'atmospheric system'.

In January 1844 *The Illustrated London News* declared atmospheric propulsion on railways to be 'an accomplished fact'. Indeed, the merits of this novel form of traction were already there to see on the Dublin & Kingstown Railway in Ireland and,

Above A reconstruction of Brunel's Atmospheric Railway, using a segment of the original piping, at Didcot Railway Centre.
Wikimedia Commons

nearer to home, on the London & Croydon line. Brunel's enthusiastic report urged the incorporation of the atmospheric system on the SDR as the means of overcoming the railway's gradients and curves.

The origins of atmospheric propulsion can be traced back to 1810 and a number of inventors who dabbled with the idea, but it was not until 1839 that the principle was further refined and patented by brothers Jacob and Joseph Samuda. Put simply, a 15in cast-iron pipe was laid between the running rails, inside which was a piston. The piston inside the pipe was connected to the framing of the leading railway carriage, in place of a locomotive, and a continuous slot sealed by a greased leather flap enabled the piston (and the carriage) to travel the entire length of the railway line. At intervals along the line, engine houses were built to accommodate air pumps which were linked to the cast-iron pipe and created a partial vacuum inside it in front of the piston. The effect of the higher pressure of the atmospheric air behind the piston caused it to be propelled along the pipe, taking the carriage with it. Perfectly fine in theory, in practice it turned out to be a disaster.

Problems with the construction of seven tunnels (totalling more than 4,700ft in length) and the sea walls along the SDR's

Left A watercolour of the Atmospheric Railway, by an unknown artist. Beneath the leading carriage can be seen the 15in cast-iron vacuum pipe between the running rails, while on the right is one of the many lineside engine houses accommodating the pumps that created the vacuum necessary for atmospheric propulsion.

4-mile coastal section between Dawlish Warren and Teignmouth caused delays to the railway's planned schedules, and it was not until 30 May 1846, a year later than forecast, that the 15 miles of line between Exeter and Teignmouth were opened for passenger traffic, operated by conventional steam locomotives hired from the GWR. Sadly, the infrastructure was not the only aspect of the undertaking in which Brunel experienced difficulties, the atmospheric system itself falling foul of air leakage from the iron pipe, deterioration of the leather flap (due to weathering and rodent damage) and repeated breakdowns in the engine houses.

It was not until September 1847 that atmospheric trains carried passengers between Exeter and Teignmouth, the service being extended to Newton Abbot the following January. But the line proved to be unworkable using atmospheric propulsion, and in September 1848 the idea was abandoned on the SDR, and the equipment sold for scrap. Steam locomotives took over the running of the services.

The 'Atmospheric Caper', as it was dubbed by locals, was a serious slur on the professional reputation of Brunel and cost the SDR and its shareholders dearly.

What's left today?

All that remains of this misguided adventure is the Italianate pumping station at Starcross, eight miles south of Exeter. The building is in a poor state of repair, its Listed status notwithstanding. For several years it housed the modest Atmospheric Railway Museum, but sadly this closed in 1993, whereupon the building was purchased by the Starcross Fishing & Cruising Club, for use as a boat store and club house. Some 200 yards from the pumping station, opposite the railway station, stands the Atmospheric Railway Inn, and on the walls of the bar are photographs, plans and drawings charting the history of Brunel's 'Atmospheric Caper'.

Clifton Suspension Bridge, Bristol (1831–64)

Perhaps the most spectacular of Brunel's bridges is that spanning the Avon Gorge at Bristol between Clifton Down and Leigh Woods.

Whether viewed from the Portway, far below, soaring high overhead against the sky, or from the pedestrian's viewpoint walking the 627ft across its slender span strung across the great chasm of the Avon Gorge, to perceive the Clifton Suspension Bridge is a truly unforgettable experience.

Although opened to the public in 1864, some five years after Brunel's death, its origins can be traced back more than 100 years, to 1754. In this year a wealthy Bristol wine merchant named William Vick left a legacy of £1,000 to the Society of Merchant Venturers for the purpose of building a stone bridge, toll-free, across the Avon Gorge from Clifton Down. He had estimated the cost at about £10,000, and by 1830 the sum invested had realised £8,000.

In order to give sufficient clearance to the tall masts of the many ships that sailed to and from Bristol's docks the bridge needed to be a very high structure, for which stone would have

Above Viewed from Brunel's South Entrance Lock, Clifton Suspension Bridge soars above the River Avon, linking Clifton Down on the right with Leigh Woods on the left. *Author*

Left A singularly impracticable design of 1793 for a stone bridge across the Avon Gorge at Clifton, designed by the aptly named William Bridges. *Author's collection*

Right This design was submitted by J.M. Rendel in 1830, in the first competition for an iron bridge across the Avon Gorge. In common with the designs submitted by other hopefuls, including Brunel, it was rejected by the Bridge Committee. *Author's collection*

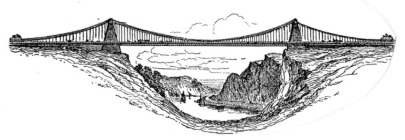

Below Thomas Telford's design was submitted at the invitation of the Bridge Committee after the others had all been rejected. His reputation as a bridge builder had been secured by his design for the impressive Menai Suspension Bridge at Anglesey, but this did not prevent his design for the Avon Gorge being rejected by the committee, on cost grounds. *Author's collection*

been an unsuitable building material, but the use of iron meant that a bridge spanning the gorge became a realistic possibility. Land was bought at Leigh Woods, and 1829 the recently formed Bridge Committee announced a competition to find a suitable design. Additional funds for the building programme were to be raised by subscription.

Of the 22 designs submitted to the Bridge Committee in November 1829, those of Brunel and four others were shortlisted. However, all were dismissed by the competition judge, Thomas

Above Telford's suspension bridge across the Menai Strait, which measures 550ft between the supporting piers, pictured against the stunning backdrop of a snow-capped Snowdonia. *Author*

Specification for Clifton Suspension Bridge, as completed in 1864

Height above high water	245ft
Span of chains (between centrelines of piers)	702ft 3in
Span between abutments	627ft
Width of deck	30ft
Weight of bridge structure	1,500 tons
Load-bearing capability	7,000 tons
Total links in chains	4,200, each 24ft long 7in wide
Height of bridge pillars	86ft
Handrail	oak
Carriage road (with transversely laid plank floor)	Baltic timber, braced together, covered
Estimated cost	£52,000
Actual cost	in excess of £100,000
Work begun	July 1831
Bridge opened	December 1864

Telford, the distinguished bridge-builder and engineer, on the grounds of impracticality. The 72-year-old engineer himself was then invited by the committee to submit a design of his own, which he duly did, but this in turn was rejected by the Merchant Venturers, on grounds of cost. Thus it was that a new competition was held in October 1830, Brunel submitting a new design, with a reduced span, which, after much lobbying of the prevaricating Bridge Committee, was accepted. Work began apace, and the first turf on the land for the bridge approaches was turned on 21 July 1831.

Brunel envisaged a single-span suspension bridge slung between two supporting towers built in the then popular Egyptian style on two huge stone abutments. Each tower was to be decorated with a pair of sphinxes, and cast-iron panels would tell the story of the bridge's construction. The bridge deck was to be suspended by 162 iron rods hanging from two massive triple-layer iron chains anchored at each end in tunnels beyond the approach roads.

Inevitable legal wrangling over land purchase, a shortage of capital (when it became apparent that less than half the £52,000

Below The date is November 1862, and work has begun on erecting the staging around the tower on the Clifton Down side of the Avon Gorge.
Bristol Museum

estimated cost of the scheme was available) and the violent Bristol Riots in October 1831 caused the suspension of all work, construction being resumed only in 1836, when the foundation stone of the Leigh Woods abutment was laid. By 1840 the two piers had been completed, and work continued until 1843, when a halt was called once more, this time due to constructional difficulties with the huge abutments on each side of the gorge and, once again, a shortage of funds, some £30,000 being needed to finish the job.

Sadly, Brunel would never see the bridge completed. The pressing need to clear some of the debts incurred thus far in its construction was addressed by the Bridge Trustees when, much to his dismay, they voted to sell off the bridge's ironwork. The two double wrought-iron suspension chains were eventually sold, in 1853, to the Cornwall Railway Co – ironically for use on Brunel's Royal Albert Bridge across the River Tamar.

In 1860, the year after Brunel's death, a new bridge company was formed with a dogged determination to push things through to a satisfactory conclusion, raising capital of £35,000. Under the guidance

Below The year 1863 saw the final phase in the construction of the bridge, with staging erected around both towers and a gangway slung between them. *Bristol Museum*

of two leading engineers of the day, Sir John Hawkshaw and William Barlow, the bridge was finally completed in 1864, although a number of structural modifications had been found necessary, and the Egyptian detailing was dropped in favour of a simpler approach. In another ironic twist to the tale Hawkshaw and Barlow were also able to use the double chains from Brunel's Hungerford Bridge in London (by now being dismantled to make way for a new railway bridge from Charing Cross station) to replace those sold 10 years previously. Although not completed precisely to Brunel's original design, the Clifton bridge nevertheless served as a fitting memorial to the great engineer, being formally opened on 8 December 1864.

Left On 8 December 1864 the opening ceremony of Clifton Suspension Bridge concluded the protracted birth of Brunel's first major civil-engineering project, albeit five years after his death. *The Illustrated London News*

Below The bridge is pictured here some 30 years after completion. *Author's collection*

Above Land chains for the bridge are anchored in caves beneath the ground, as seen here on the Clifton Down side. *Author*

Left Viewed in the direction of the Leigh Woods abutment, the deck of the bridge leaps 700ft across the chasm of the Avon Gorge. *Author*

What's left today?

Clifton Suspension Bridge remains today very much as it was when it first opened to the public 150 years ago. A potent and highly visible symbol of Bristol's industrial heritage and of Brunel's links with the city, it is still used every day by pedestrians and light road traffic.

Maidenhead Bridge, Berkshire (1838)

Maidenhead Railway Bridge was built in 1837/8 to the design of Brunel to carry the GWR over the River Thames east of Maidenhead. There were many doubters who feared that his daring design of two principal arches each with an unprecedented span of 128ft across a rise of only 25ft 3in would never stand unsupported. When the contractor removed the centring from beneath the eastern arch before the mortar had set the crown settled by 5in, appearing to vindicate Brunel's detractors. But Brunel understood the cause and ordered the replacement of the centring and repaired the arch. The following year floodwater washed away the centring, but the arches remained intact and indeed stand true to this day.

The bridge is a symmetrical structure comprising approach abutments and four semi-circular flood arches on each bank, flanking the two wide semi-elliptical arches across the river, with a pier on a mid-stream island. Brunel's solution to reduce the dynamic forces acting on the main bridge spans was to build a system of internal longitudinal walls and voids to lighten the superstructure, thereby reducing the mass of the bridge and its foundations. This also saved on materials, time and cost.

Between 1890 and 1893 the bridge was widened by Sir John Fowler, acting as a consultant to the GWR, to accommodate four tracks. Extensions – with elevations that exactly matched Brunel's originals – were added to both sides of the existing structure, these being closely piled in order to prevent any differential settling.

What's left today?

There have been no significant alterations to the bridge since the late 19th century, and despite the widening it looks very much the same as it did when Brunel built it. Dozens of high-speed trains pass over it every day.

Devil's Bridge, Bleadon, Somerset (1841)

This single-span brick over-bridge crosses the former Bristol & Exeter railway line between Weston-super-Mare and Burnham-on-Sea. It is said to be highest single-span bridge on the line.

What's left today?

The bridge remains in use today, allowing local traffic to cross the Great Western main line.

Above Devil's Bridge at Bleadon Hill, near Weston-super-Mare. *Geof Sheppard*

Hungerford Bridge, London (1844/5)

Although dismantled in 1862, just three years after his death, Brunel's impressive suspension bridge over the River Thames in Central London deserves particular mention here, for an interesting reason. In order to replace the chains from the Clifton Suspension Bridge that were sold to the Cornwall Railway in 1853 when the Clifton scheme ran into financial difficulties, the chains from Hungerford Bridge were acquired upon the latter's dismantling, for the paltry sum of £5,000.

Not unlike the Clifton bridge in appearance, Hungerford Bridge was designed as a pedestrian crossing linking Lambeth, on the south bank of the Thames, with Hungerford Market, on the north side. Two 80ft-high brick piers, built in the river to an Italianate campanile style, carried the bridge platform 1,352ft across the Thames, suspended from four iron suspension chains. *The Illustrated London News* observed that pedestrians could 'walk through the centre of the fruit stalls, over the fish market, and in a few minutes find themselves in Pedlar's Acre, Lambeth'.

What's left today?

Today it is still possible to cross the river by a bridge at this point, be it on foot or by rail, but the market has gone, buried under Charing Cross station. On the Lambeth side, beyond the South Bank complex and Jubilee Gardens, is Belvedere Road, once known as Pedlar's Acre. All that remains of Brunel's elegant suspension bridge are the foundations of the brick piers which carry the railway across

Above and right
When opened on 1 May 1845 Brunel's elegant Hungerford Suspension Bridge provided pedestrians with a crossing over the Thames from Hungerford market to Pedlar's Acre, on the south bank. In 1862 it was pulled down to make way for a railway bridge across the river. This historic early photograph was taken by William Henry Fox-Talbot. Hungerford and Golden Jubilee bridges can be seen today behind the London Eye.
Author's collection/Ian Black

Specification for Hungerford Bridge, as completed in 1845

Height above water (middle of centre span)	32½ft
Height above water (near piers)	28½ft
Span between abutments	1,352ft
Length of central span	676ft
Width of deck	14ft
Height of piers	80ft
Weight of suspension chains	715 tons
Total links in chains	2,600 (each 24ft long and 7in wide)
Cost of brickwork	£63,000
Cost of ironwork	£17,000
Total construction cost	£106,000
Work began	1844
Opened to public	1 May 1845

the Thames from Charing Cross station to Waterloo on the new Hungerford Bridge (1864), designed by Sir John Hawkshaw. In 2002 a pair of cable-stayed pedestrian bridges were opened on either side of the railway bridge; sharing the same foundation piers, they are known as the Golden Jubilee Bridges.

Royal Albert Bridge, Saltash, Cornwall (1848–59)

Although lacking the grace and finesse of his Clifton Suspension Bridge, Brunel's design for the Royal Albert Bridge linking Devon with Cornwall across the Tamar at Saltash is by any standard an imposing piece of civil engineering. In order to facilitate the expansion into Cornwall of Brunel's broad-gauge railway a bridge of more than 1,100ft in span was needed. In May 1859 *The Illustrated London News* highlighted the great difficulties that were faced in the bridge's construction and paid tribute to its designer: 'Mr Brunel is the engineer to whom is due the merit of having overcome these difficulties; and the Albert Viaduct [*sic*] is another example of his great mechanical genius.'

Drawing upon experience gained in the design and construction of his reconstructed Usk Viaduct, the Thames bridge at Windsor and the bridge over the River Wye at Chepstow, Brunel envisaged a double-span bridge supported mid-river on a central iron pier with a stone base, each span measuring 465ft. As with his bridge at Clifton, Brunel had to allow sufficient clearance for shipping passing beneath at high water. The two main spans incorporated the three classic elements of bridge construction – a beam forming the deck structure, connected to a system arches and chains. The twin elliptical tubular arches were made of cast iron and measured 16ft 9in wide and 12ft 4in deep. Almost half of the chains used to suspend the deck from the arches had been made more than 20 years previously for the Clifton Suspension Bridge. The Tamar bridge itself was to be linked to the land at each end by a series of tall stone piers supporting an iron deck carrying a single railway track.

Some 175 preliminary borings into the riverbed's sub-strata were made during 1847 to find the optimum point at which to sink foundations for the central pier. However, due to a lack of capital the Cornwall Railway Co suspended all work for more than three years.

Below The second tubular span of the Royal Albert Bridge at Saltash is readied for raising into place in July 1858.

Specification for the Royal Albert Bridge, as completed in 1859

Height of platform above high water	100ft
Greatest height from foundation to summit	260ft
Overall length of platform	2,200ft
Each span	455ft long, 56ft deep, 1,060 tons in weight
Number of approach spans	17 (eight Devon side, nine Cornwall side)
Central pier	Four octagonal cast-iron columns, 96ft high
Central pier foundations	Stone base 96ft deep, founded on riverbed, the upper 50ft measuring 37ft in diameter, the lower 46ft being of 35ft diameter
Materials used in construction	c2,650 tons wrought iron, c1,200 tons cast iron, 14,000cu ft timber, 459,000cu ft stonework
Total cost	£225,000
Work began	1847
Bridge opened	2 May 1859

Left Due to his failing health Brunel was not present at the opening of his Royal Albert Bridge by Prince Albert, the Prince Consort, in May 1859. *The Illustrated London News*

When work resumed in 1853 Brunel employed a device he and his father had used on the Thames Tunnel at Rotherhithe during the 1830s. This consisted of an iron cylinder, measuring 35ft in diameter at its base, with a complex series of internal compartments, fed with compressed air, which was lowered into position midstream to enable workmen to lay the underwater foundations of the central pier in the dry. By the end of 1856 the foundations had been completed.

Wrought-iron trusses for the two central spans were fabricated next to the riverbank, and the first was floated out into position on a pontoon on 1 September 1857, under the supervision of Brunel himself. The second was floated in July the following year, the operation being supervised this time by Brunel's principal assistant, R.P. Brereton. The trusses were secured in place and over the coming months were jacked up 3ft at a time to their final positions by hydraulic presses as the stonework was built up beneath them and on the land piers at each end. The bridge was finally ready to receive traffic in May 1859, but sadly Brunel was too ill to attend the official opening by Prince Albert, who travelled down from London by train. Instead Brunel viewed his last great bridging achievement whilst lying on a specially converted platform truck, hauled very slowly across the bridge by one of Daniel Gooch's locomotives.

What's left today?

The bridge still stands tall and proud over the River Tamar, carrying a single rail track upon which trains observe a speed restriction to ensure that the bridge structure is not subjected to more stress than is necessary.

Regular maintenance of the bridge is undertaken by Network Rail, and in recent years replacements, modifications and strengthening have been carried out on the bridge's deck, hangers and bracing components. Thanks to careful monitoring of its condition it is expected to have many more years of useful life. A suspension bridge for road traffic was built parallel to the Royal Albert Bridge in the 1960s, and from this it is possible to obtain a good view of Brunel's grand structure.

Thames Bridge, Windsor, Berkshire (1849)

Although at 203ft in span considerably smaller than the bridges described hitherto, the wrought-iron bowstring girder bridge spanning the Thames at Windsor is significant in that it represents the oldest surviving example of one of Brunel's wrought-iron bridges. Designed to carry the branch from the GWR main line at Slough across the River Thames to Windsor, it was approached from the Slough side on a low timber viaduct supporting a double track.

What's left today?

The timber viaduct has since been replaced by brick structures, and the track is now single.

Chepstow Bridge, Monmouthshire (1849–52)

When Brunel's iron bridge across the River Wye at Chepstow was opened to rail traffic on 19 July 1852 it completed the final link in the South Wales Railway between Gloucester and Swansea. The

Below When the railway bridge at Chepstow was built in 1852 it comprised four spans – a single river span and three land spans carrying twin railway decks. The unusual lie of the land was a challenge to Brunel, and his design solution at Chepstow was put to good use when later he took on the far greater challenge of bridging the Tamar. *Author's collection*

Above The pillars and stone abutment of Brunel's Chepstow railway bridge are all that remain of the original structure.
Andy Dingley

river channel at Chepstow has one of the highest tidal ranges in the world, and this prompted the Admiralty to stipulate that any bridge over the Wye should consist of a single span with a navigable headway of 50ft above the highest tide. The location of the proposed bridge posed another problem in that the east bank of the river is a high rocky cliff whereas the west bank is a mud flat.

When built in 1852 the bridge comprised of four spans – a single river span of 300ft and three land spans of 100ft. Twin railway decks carrying the tracks (only one track being operational initially, the second coming into use on 18 April 1853) were suspended from diagonal chains hung from two 9ft-diameter wrought-iron tubes. Fabricated on the river foreshore using the riveted-plate construction method common to shipbuilding and steam boilers at that time, these tubes were then floated into position on barges and jacked into position, resting on a pair of stone towers on the Gloucester side and corresponding towers of cast-iron plates supported by six cylinders in the river.

The horizontal girders of the three land spans were renewed in 1948 after partial collapse, but the river span was dismantled and replaced in 1962 by welded trusses.

What's left today?

The bridge continues to carry rail traffic, but the piers beneath the land spans and the massive southwest abutment are the only remnants of Brunel's original design.

Balmoral Bridge, Braemar, Aberdeenshire (1857)

In 1854 Brunel was commissioned by Prince Albert to design a bridge as part of improvements to the Balmoral Estate, replacing the nearby Crathie suspension bridge as the main vehicular access across the River Dee to Balmoral.

The structure is a single-span wrought-iron plate girder bridge, slightly cambered, with regularly pierced iron plate parapets and distinctive visible riveting. It has coursed rock-face granite abutments with capped square granite piers and curved granite approach walls at either end. Five roller-bearings were incorporated

Below Balmoral Bridge is probably the least attractive of all Brunel's bridges.

into the design beneath the mounted ends of the girders at the east end of the bridge, together with an innovative girder section designed to resist buckling. The bridge can support a load of 86 tons, sufficient to bear the weight of modern traffic.

The final appearance of this rather plain bridge did not entirely meet with the approval of its Royal patrons. Queen Victoria was apparently not amused by its lack of ornamentation, a pattern of diagonal web plates along the parapets, punctuated with cross-beams every 15ft, providing the only decorative element. Brunel, however, was proud of his design of 'functional elegance'.

What's left today?
Over the years the bridge has undergone several phases of alteration and repair, the most recent being a comprehensive conservation programme in 2012 that included replacement of the decayed timber deck with modern equivalent in composite steel and reinforced-concrete.

Augustus Way Bridge, Brentford, Middlesex (1859)

Constructed in 1859 to link Brunel's Brentford Dock with the GWR at Southall, the wrought-iron plate girder bridge is a typical Brunel design and was one of several built as part of the Great Western, Brentford & Thames Junction Railway. The transverse deck beams were replaced (probably in the early 20th century) when extra stiffeners were added, and connection details upgraded. Today pre-cast pre-stressed concrete slabs support the roadway.

What's left today?
Brentford Dock closed in 1964, and the track was lifted in the 1970s, whereupon the trackbed was used for a road (Augustus Way) and the bridge converted to carry motor traffic over The Ham, an existing riverside road.

Cornish railway viaducts (1859–89)

The broad-gauge route to Penzance, along with its branch lines, presented a particular challenge to Brunel, in that there was a need to span dozens of deep and narrow valleys characteristic of South Devon and Cornwall but little money to pay for them.

Above Replacing Brunel's 756ft-long structure in stone and timber, the nine-arch stone viaduct at Carnon, in west Cornwall, carries the railway from Truro to Falmouth over the Carnon river valley. The original stone piers remain *in situ* alongside the newer structure. *Geof Sheppard*

Left Some 147ft high and 947ft in length, Moorswater Viaduct, west of Liskeard, was probably the most spectacular of Brunel's Cornish viaducts. *Author's collection*

Capital was simply not available for financing the construction of stone or wrought-iron viaducts, because the railway companies concerned were unlikely to generate the requisite level of traffic when compared with those serving the more populous counties. Brunel's solution was to design and build timber viaducts, which became prominent and numerous features of the landscape in the South West of England. There were 42 in total, with a combined length of four miles, 34 of them being found between Plymouth and Truro alone. These tall, gangling structures presented dramatic man-made statements in the ancient Cornish landscape, the tallest, at St Pinnock, near Liskeard, towering some 153ft high.

All the viaducts in Devon and Cornwall were built from high-quality yellow pine sourced from Memel in the Baltic (in present-day Lithuania). Structures carrying the railway across tidal creeks used timber trestles founded on piles to support the superstructure, with heavy timbers radiating upwards to bear the platform carrying the track, while those inland were carried on tall stone-built piers. These viaducts had a life-expectancy of 30 years, but some lasted for as long as 60, which made them an attractive economic proposition. Those along the main line to Penzance were replaced in 1908 when the track was doubled. In any case, by the end of the 19th century Baltic pine had become unobtainable; the substitute wood (Oregon pine) had a much shorter lifespan, which made replacing timber with timber uneconomic, thus sounding the death-knell for Cornwall's wooden viaducts. By 1931 only three remained, and these were replaced shortly afterwards.

What's left today?

Many of Brunel's wooden structures have long since been replaced by stone piers and steel girder bridges which continue to carry rail traffic, an example being that at Liskeard. Others are ghosts of their former selves, among them the crumbling piers of the original Moorswater Viaduct, which stand beside the later (1881) structure carrying the main line west to Penzance.

Loughor Viaduct, Glamorgan (1852)

Built in 1852, the Loughor railway viaduct in South Wales was one of Brunel's numerous timber viaducts. The 750ft-long, 18-span timber trestle structure carried a single-track railway line over the Loughor Estuary between Swansea and Llanelli. A 40ft opening swing bridge was incorporated at the Swansea (eastern) end to allow river traffic to pass.

Over the years the viaduct's superstructure has benefited from substantial re-designs and strengthening works. It was rebuilt in 1880 when the original wooden spans were replaced with wrought-iron girders supported on the original trestles while in 1907 major reconstruction saw the swing-bridge span dismantled and the abutments rebuilt in stone, new trestles being driven and a timber deck added. The most recent refurbishment was carried out between 1979 and 1981, when the trestles were reconfigured by detaching the outer timbers and reusing them as sloping stays to improve the viaduct's lateral stability.

What's left today?

In the early 21st century detailed site investigations and conditional surveys concluded that the viaduct had reached the end of its life. In April 2013 Network Rail and contractor Carillion replaced the entire structure, including the existing piers within the current track alignment, with a new viaduct capable of supporting two tracks, as part of the larger £50 million Gowerton re-doubling scheme.

Below Replacement of the Loughor Viaduct with a modern steel structure. Some of the original wooden piling has been left as a reminder of its Brunel origins. *The Rail Engineer*

8 CONSERVING BRUNEL'S LEGACY

Brunel's structures have become synonymous with the landscapes and places where they can be found, be it the string of lofty viaducts striding across the Cornish valleys or the ribbon of the Great Western Railway line threading its way across England from east to west.

We value these structures for reasons other their mere functional use, and as 'heritage assets' they have a value far beyond their pecuniary worth. Future generations will most likely value them too, for the same reasons, so we have a duty to care for them before passing them on to our children and their children after them.

Given our strong sense of pride in our national heritage, you would think that such treasures would be safe and secure from despoliation by those who would tear them down and raise sprawling housing estates or office blocks in their place. You would be wrong.

Above Brunel's first iron bridge over the Grand Union Canal in London, was hidden within a modern brick bridge. It was discovered on the eve of the bridge being demolished. *Press Association (PA-1896090)*

Paddington's fourth span saved from demolition

In 2003, with the full backing of English Heritage, Network Rail applied to demolish the fourth span of Paddington station's trainshed 'to create a station that meets passenger demand, provides better access, and improves the interchange with other transport'. The fourth span was an Edwardian addition to Brunel's

original three trainsheds, but it was carefully designed to match. What Network Rail failed to mention was that demolition would also deliver a massive commercial return, with thousands of square feet of new shops and a large office development on a deck over the tracks. The demolition of this Grade I Listed structure had the full backing of Westminster City Council, the Commission for Architecture and the Built Environment, English Heritage and the Victorian Society.

Above Span 4 at Paddington was saved from demolition by Network Rail. *Author*

A passionate and ultimately successful campaign for preservation of the fourth span was waged against Network Rail and its allies by architectural historians. Had demolition gone ahead it would have been the most extensive destruction of a Grade I structure since listing began – a return to the bad old days of the 1960s. In 2006 Network Rail was forced to abandon its plans and restore the structure to facilitate construction of Crossrail's infrastructure.

The rediscovery and salvage of Brunel's 'lost' Bishop's Road canal bridge

Steven Brindle, Inspector of Ancient Monuments for English Heritage, was researching a new history of Paddington station when he came across evidence at the National Archives of a previously unrecognised iron bridge by Brunel, built over the canal at

Paddington in 1839. It was the engineer's first iron bridge and had a unique design. Rebuilding work in 1906 had obscured the original structure and caused it to become lost from view.

By good fortune the bridge was rediscovered only months before major redevelopment work around Paddington station and Bishop's Road Bridge would have seen its demolition in 2004. If this important new find were to be saved then a plan would have to be hatched – and fast. Discussions between Westminster City Council, English Heritage and the contractors enabled the 35ft-span Brunel cast-iron girder bridge to be dismantled for removal on 31 March and 1 April 2004, allowing the Bishop's Road bridge-replacement work to proceed as planned.

At the time of writing the dismantled bridge is being stored by English Heritage at Fort Cumberland, near Portsmouth. Westminster City Council and British Waterways have identified a site for rebuilding the bridge, for pedestrian use, some 200 yards up the canal from its original location, close by the Harrow Road. This means the bridge will still relate meaningfully to its original setting and will serve a genuine need for a footbridge.

The conflicting agendas of preservation and running a 21st-century railway – the GWR main line and the UNESCO World Heritage Site bid

In 1998 excitement was in the air after it was announced that the Great Western main line was under consideration for listing as a UNESCO World Heritage Site. The proposal came from Bath Heritage Watchdog for 'The Great Western World Heritage Site – the Genesis of Modern Transport' and comprised seven individual sites – Bristol Temple Meads railway station (including Brunel's company offices, boardroom and trainshed, the Bristol & Exeter Railway offices and the main line over the River Avon), Bath Spa railway station (along with the main line from Twerton Tunnel to Sydney Gardens), Middle Hill and Box tunnels, the Swindon area (including Swindon Works and the Railway Village), Maidenhead Bridge, Wharncliffe Viaduct and Paddington station.

In the bid for inclusion on the 'UK Tentative List of Potential Sites for World Heritage Nomination' the GWR was described as 'a string of pearls loosely linked by the line of the railway containing further beads, which provide context but not forming part of the site itself', while 'At either end [were] Paddington

station, London, and Temple Meads, Bristol – Brunel's magnificent railway termini – and the Great Western Dock with the SS *Great Britain* in Bristol's floating harbour.'

Key points made in the submission emphasised that, unlike other earlier or contemporary railways, the GWR main line had been operating as such for 170 years and was one of the most complete still in everyday use, most of its buildings and structures surviving intact; moreover it was the creation of just one individual, Brunel, embracing his vision in the fields of architecture, structural, civil and mechanical engineering, and these significant innovations were what the Great Western World Heritage Site sought to recognise, together with the genius of the man himself.

The initiative gathered momentum, and with a declaration by then Culture Secretary Chris Smith that the London–Bristol line was 'a masterpiece of human creative genius' the omens for inclusion on the UK Tentative list seemed favourable.

At about the same time as the Great Western World Heritage Site bid the Government announced the intended electrification of the GWR main line. The method chosen, with its gantries and overhead power cables, along with supporting infrastructure, was likely to have a pronounced visual (and possibly structural) impact on the landscape traversed by the GWR, especially so in a sensitive setting like the 18th-century Sydney Gardens, on the

Above Electrification was introduced west of Paddington station in 1998 with the opening of the Heathrow Express service between the London terminus and Heathrow Airport. The Government intends to electrify the entire Great Western main line as far west as Cardiff by 2017. This is Hanwell station, with an HST passing through at speed beneath the 25kV AC overhead catenary. *Brian Morrison*

Above Sydney Gardens, Bath.

eastern outskirts of Bath. The much less intrusive third-rail (DC) option was ruled out by Network Rail because it would limit line speeds to no more than 110mph and would cost 20% more to operate than an overhead (AC) network.

As it happened, submissions by the City of Liverpool, the Pontcysyllte aqueduct in Wales and the Cornish mining sites succeeded in making it onto the official UK Tentative list, but the GWR – along with a host of other bids – fell by the wayside. The Independent Expert Panel's report to the Department for Culture, Media & Sport in March 2011 opined that the 'string-of-pearls' approach did not adequately represent the significance of the GWR, stating: 'There was confusion over whether the proposal focused on the railway or Brunel. The opposition of the principal owner [Network Rail] was insuperable.'

Cynics might be forgiven for concluding that the forthcoming electrification of the line between London and Bristol, planned for 2016/7 and worth billions of pounds in contracts, was the reason that the GWR bid never made it onto the shortlist for World Heritage status. The question of whether the heritage of the GWR was worth listing came a long way behind protecting the Government's policy on electrification of the line, or so it might seem to some.

Railway historians and enthusiasts live in hope that one day the entire GWR will become a World Heritage Site, but at the time of writing (2014) the Government has yet to make a formal proposal to UNESCO. And the chances are that there will be a long wait before it feels inclined to do so.

There are always two sides to an argument, and it is tempting to ponder what Brunel would have done, faced with the dilemma of upgrading the existing railway network or leaving it alone to stagnate. The arguments for electrification are persuasive: electric trains create far less environmental pollution than do diesel locomotives and are cheaper to maintain, they weigh significantly less than the ageing HSTs they are replacing (and will therefore cause less damage to existing structures like track, bridges and viaducts), and electric traction offers higher line speeds and frequency of services, leading to shorter journey times – typically Bath to London in one hour. The likelihood is that Brunel would have embraced the new technology but that he would also have found innovative ways of minimising its visual impact on the landscape.

There can be little doubt that electrification of the GWR main line will go ahead, but it is hoped that the Government and Network Rail will respect the integrity of one of the world's most perfectly formed historic inter-city transport networks.

One positive development in 2014 has been in the number of structures along the GWR that have been newly accorded Listed status or have been upgraded – one station (the modest stone building on the island platform at Swindon), four viaducts, 12 tunnel structures and 26 bridges – such that the previous total has all but doubled. Notable among the newly Listed structures is Box Tunnel, between Chippenham and Bath.

The Mechanics' Institute at Swindon – a national treasure in jeopardy

Built 1853-5 by Edward Roberts and paid for by rail workers, the Grade II* Listed Mechanics' Institute occupies Emlyn Square, in the centre of Brunel's Railway Village at Swindon. In its heyday it contained the UK's first lending library and also opened up health services to other workers. Aneurin Bevan, founder of the NHS, said: 'There was a complete health service in Swindon. All we had to do was expand it to the country.'

After it closed in 1986 the Institute fell prey to vandals and arsonists. Years of neglect by its owners and a lack of decisive leadership by Swindon Borough Council led in 2012 to the Institute's being placed on the Victorian Society's register of top 10 endangered

Right The Mechanics' Institute in Emlyn Square, Swindon, remains under threat from neglect. *Author*

historic buildings. In 2014 the Institute is owned by the Crown Estate, but the long-term future of this nationally important building remains undecided, and its condition continues to deteriorate.

Brunel pumping station at Totnes saved from demolition by its owner

Brunel's pumping station at Totnes, Devon, a survivor of the his Atmospheric Railway experiment of the 1840s, faced demolition as a result of plans by Dairy Crest to level the site and sell it off after closing its creamery business in 2007.

Below Public pressure forced English Heritage to list the Brunel pumping station at Totnes, saving it from destruction.
Geof Sheppard

The Department for Culture, Media & Sport, on the advice of English Heritage, refused to accord the building Listed status, in contrast to the other remaining pumping stations, at Starcross and Torre. Mark Horton, the industrial archaeologist from TV's *Coast* series, said: 'Very little of our industrial heritage is now safe if this extraordinary decision is allowed to stand. English Heritage are effectively whitewashing history.'

'People power' and lobbying by prominent public figures ultimately forced English Heritage into a *volte-face*, and the pumping station was given Listed status in 2008, just in time to save it from demolition, but the question still needs to be asked as to why it took a public outcry to persuade English Heritage to live up to its declared aim 'to protect and promote England's spectacular historic environment'.

PART TWO

BRUNEL
WHAT'S LEFT
TO SEE TODAY

John Doubleday's sculpture
of Brunel (1982), pictured in
its original location on Broad
Quay in Bristol, looks towards
the city's docks, where both the
PS *Great Western* and SS *Great
Britain* were built and launched.
Author

What's left, at a glance

Below is a summary of Brunel's principal achievements that remain to be seen today:

Along the London–Bristol main line

Paddington station and Hilton London Paddington Hotel (formerly Great Western Royal Hotel)
Wharncliffe Viaduct, Hanwell, Middx
Thames Bridge, Windsor, Berks
Thames Bridge, Maidenhead, Berks (now Bucks)
Sonning Cutting, Berks
Mortimer station, Berks (on Reading–Basingstoke line)
Thames Bridge, Basildon, Berks
Thames Bridge, Moulsford, Berks (now Oxon)
Culham station, Berks (now Oxon; on Didcot–Oxford line)
Steventon, Berks (now Oxon) – District Superintendent's House
Swindon station, Wilts
Swindon Railway Village, Swindon, Wilts
Chippenham station and viaduct, Wilts
Box Tunnel, Wilts
Middlehill Tunnel, Wilts
Bath Spa station, Somerset – retaining walls and bridges in Sydney Gardens, Sydney Gardens
    East and West tunnels, St James's Bridge (east of station), Dolemeads and St James's viaducts
    (to east and west of station), Twerton Viaduct and twin tunnels
Saltford Tunnel, Saltford, Somerset
St Anne's Park Nos 2 and 3 tunnels, Bristol
Avon Bridge over river at Whitby Road, east of Temple Meads, hidden by steel rail bridges Bristol
    Temple Meads station (1878) – original terminus offices and trainshed (1840), Temple Gate, Bristol

Atmospheric Railway, Devon

Starcross, Totnes, Torre – pumping stations for railway

Larger bridges

Bleadon (Devil's Bridge), Weston-super-Mare, Somerset (rail)
Royal Albert Bridge, Saltash, Cornwall (rail)
Clifton Suspension Bridge, Bristol (vehicle/pedestrian)

Cornish viaducts (remains of)

Examples at Moorswater and St Pinnock near Liskeard station

Tunnels

Thames Tunnel between Wapping and Rotherhithe, London (London Overground)

Ships

SS *Great Britain*, Great Western Dock, Gas Ferry Road, Bristol
Prince Street Bridge, Bristol – site of Wapping Wharf, from where PS *Great Western* launched

Docks

Brunel's South Entrance Lock and tubular iron swivel bridge, Cumberland Basin, Bristol
Underfall Dam and Boatyard, Cumberland Road, Bristol
Netham Dam, Feeder Road, Bristol
Briton Ferry Dock, Neath
Brentford Dock, Brentford, Middx
Monkwearmouth (North Dock), Sunderland
Mill Bay Dock, Plymouth

Miscellaneous

Church at Church Road, Barton, Watcombe, Devon
Statue of Brunel, junction of Temple Place and Victoria Embankment,
     London (by Carlo Marochetti)
Statue of Brunel on Broad Quay, Bristol (by John Doubleday)
Statue of Brunel in Brunel Shopping Centre, Swindon, Wilts
Statue of Brunel at Paddington station, London (by John Doubleday)
Memorial window to Brunel in Westminster Abbey, London (by Norman Shaw)
Brunel family grave, Kensal Green Cemetery, London
Brunel's Tunnel House, Saltford, Somerset

Museums

Science Museum, Exhibition Road, London – various small exhibits
Bristol Museum & Art Gallery – documents, paintings and artefacts
National Railway Museum, York – photographs, documents, drawings
Steam: Museum of the GWR, Swindon, Wilts – photographs, drawings, artefacts
Railway Village, Swindon, Wilts
National Maritime Museum, Greenwich – scale model of SS *Great Britain*, documents, drawings,
     paintings, various small exhibits
Rotherhithe, London – restored engine house from Thames Tunnel, museum

Places with Brunel connections

Portsea, Portsmouth – Brunel's birthplace in Britain Street; house now demolished, commemorated
     by plaque on the site
Duke Street, London W1 – the Brunel family home at No 18 and the entire street later demolished to
     build the Colonial Office
Millwall, East London – plaque to commemorate PSS *Great Eastern*, built and launched from here
Bristol – Brunel House, behind City Hall, built with Brunel's involvement as Royal Western Hotel to
     accommodate transit passengers between the GWR and PS *Great Western*

9 BRUNEL IN BATH

How to get there

By road: M4 Jct 18, follow A46 for 10 miles to T-junction with A4 at Lambridge on outskirts of city, turn right at traffic lights and follow signs to city centre.

In common with many other cities today, parking in Bath can prove a headache. In central Bath there is heavy traffic congestion. Ever-vigilant traffic wardens and tow-away contractors are waiting to pounce on the unwary motorist who inadvertently parks in the wrong place at the wrong time. This can be inconvenient and very costly, so beware. However, the following tips will help make parking for your visit easier:

Above The skew bridge crosses the Avon to the west of Bath Spa station. It replaced Brunel's original wooden structure, of which only the central stone-built pier remains. *Author*

- Central pay-and-display car parks are situated at Avon Street, Broad Street (small), Charlotte Street, Southgate, Manvers Street, Sawclose (small) and The Podium (maximum stay 3 hours); the Sainsbury's and Homebase supermarket car parks at Green Park (off Lower Bristol Road) offer free parking if you shop at one or other of the stores.

- On-street parking is expensive; purchase a ticket from parking meter.

- Outer zones restricted to 1 or 2 hours. If you like exercise you can park without restriction in the suburbs and walk to your destination.

- Park-and-ride from Newbridge (Bristol side, service 21), Lansdown (north side, service 41), Odd Down (south side, service 41) and Bath University (Saturdays only).

By rail: Frequent main-line services to Bath Spa (telephone National Rail Enquiries on 0871 200 4950 or see website www.nationalrail.co.uk) from London, Cardiff, Bristol and the South Coast.

By bus or coach: Frequent bus and express coach services to Dorchester Street Bus & Coach Station (www.firstgroup.com/ukbus/bristol_bath) from most towns and cities nationwide.

Bath Spa railway station

Manvers Street, Bath BA1 1SU

How to get there

On foot: Leave Bath Bus & Coach Station and turn right. The railway station now faces you at the end of the street.

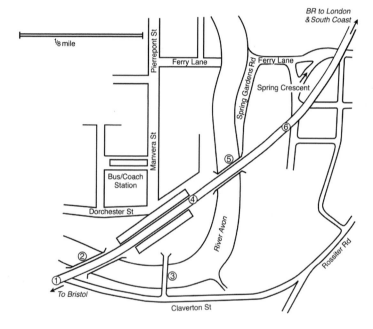

Left Map of Brunel structures in central Bath.

1. St James' viaduct
2. Skew bridge
3. Halfpenny bridge (not Brunelian)
4. Bath Spa station
5. St James' bridge
6. Dolemeads viaduct

Left The Brunel Brasserie at the Royal Hotel in Bath, opposite Bath Spa railway station. *Author*

Attractions to the west of the station

Twin-span timber-arch 'skew' bridge (site of)

With your back to the station turn right past the parcel and left-luggage office, turn right again and walk through the tunnel under the station to Halfpenny Bridge beyond. Stand on the bridge and look to your right to see where the modern skew bridge spans the river further downstream.

Brunel's original timber bridge comprised two arches, each of 80ft and composed of six ribs springing from the abutment and from a central stone pier. The whole was held together by bolts, iron straps, cross struts and ties. In 1878 the wooden bridge was replaced which, in turn, has been replaced by the bridge visible today.

Below The skew bridge and the viaduct are linked by this impressive neo-Tudor/Gothic façade overlooking the south bank of the Avon. *Author*

St James's Viaduct (73 arches, 1,800ft)

Cross Halfpenny Bridge and turn right, following the river for 250yd with the main road (Claverton Street) to your left. Pass under the viaduct to your right and cross the footbridge. The best views can be had from the Churchill road bridge further downstream and from Oak Street just past the petrol station on the A4 Lower Bristol Road. Originally the viaduct was faced with

Bath stone, but over the years this has been largely replaced by more durable brick.

Twerton Viaduct (1,914ft)

Follow the A4 along the Lower Bristol Road for 1½ miles in the direction of Bristol. Shortly after the disused Herman Miller factory at the bottom of Lansdown View, on the left can be seen the Twerton Viaduct running parallel with the main road for ½ mile.

Twerton tunnels (135ft and 792ft)

Continue along the Lower Bristol Road for ¾ mile as far as the traffic lights at its junction with the dual carriageway at Newbridge. Turn up the trackway on the left immediately before the traffic lights. The western portal of Twerton Long Tunnel can be seen to the left from the stone bridge over the railway line.

Attractions to the east of the station

St James's Bridge

Cross Halfpenny Bridge and turn left along the main road and left again after 100yd to follow the riverside path. You will see St James's Bridge straight ahead carrying the railway line over the River Avon. Much repair work in brick is evident, replacing the less resilient Bath stone.

Dolemeads Viaduct (765ft)

Walk under St James's Bridge and turn right to walk alongside the arches of the Dolemeads viaduct. (In the latter part of the 19th century the Dolemeads was one of Bath's most notorious slum areas and suffered badly from flooding from the nearby River Avon.) You will shortly find yourself in Spring Crescent where you should turn left and follow the road to eventually join Ferry Lane. Pass under the railway bridge and proceed to the main road ahead.

Sydney Gardens – Brunel bridges and cutting

Cross over the main road (Pulteney Road), turn left and follow it under the new railway bridge. Continue past the traffic lights and proceed along Pulteney Road for about 300yd, passing the County Hotel on your left, until you reach the roundabout. Cross the road at the bottom of Bathwick Hill on your right, passing St Mary's Church on your right before walking along Darlington Street. Take the next

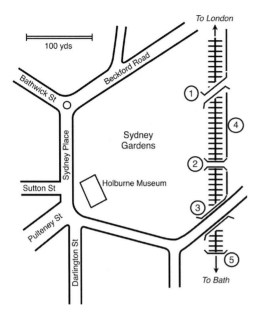

1. Stone footbridge
2. Iron footbridge
3. Sydney Road bridge
4. Brick and stone facing retaining wall
5. Sydney Gardens East and West tunnels

Above Map of Brunel structures to be found in Sydney Gardens.

Right Tunnel House in Saltford. The railway tunnel was built directly beneath this property.
Jon Godfrey

turning on your right into Sydney Place then cross over the road. Sydney Gardens is now in front of you. By following the main pathway bearing to the right you will soon find yourself alongside the railway line, with the Bath stone and brick-faced cutting ahead of you, the pedestrian Bath stone and iron bridges spanning the railway line to your left, and the Bath stone and brick Sydney Road Bridge to your right.

Attractions west of Bath

Tunnel House

Norman Road, Saltford, Bath, BS31 3BF

This elegant mid-18th-century three-storey house was named Tunnel House when the Saltford railway tunnel for the GWR was built directly beneath it. The property was purchased by Brunel in April 1836 and conveyed to the GWR in December 1837. In recent years the house has been used as a guest house and hotel, but it is now a private family home.

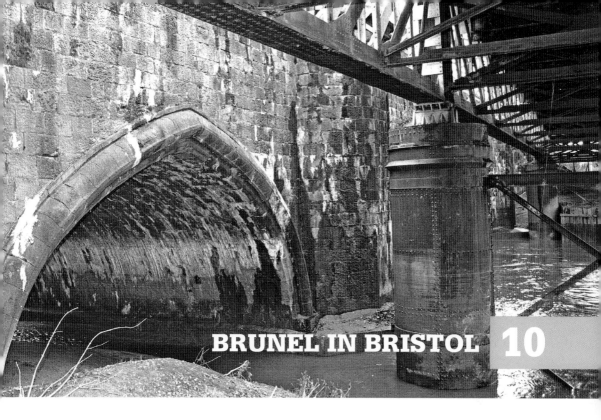

BRUNEL IN BRISTOL 10

How to get there

By road: M4 Jct 19 then M32 to city centre; M5 Jct 16 and A38 to city centre, Jct 17 and A4018 to Clifton, or Jct 18 and A4 to Cumberland Basin. A frequent park-and-ride service operates daily from the A4 at Brislington on the Bath side of the city.

By rail: Frequent mainline services to Bristol Temple Meads at Temple Gate (tel: 0871 200 4950), from London Paddington, the South Coast, the South West, Wales and the North.

By bus or coach: Frequent services to Central Bus Station in Marlborough Street (tel: 0870 888 1710) from many towns and cities nationwide.

Above On the outskirts of Bristol, in the vicinity of Arno's Vale, the railway once more crosses the Avon. The bridge pictured here is one of only two on the entire Great Western line in the Gothic style. It was built with three arches, of which the central span reaches 100ft across the river. *Author*

Netham Dam and Weir
Whitby Road, Bristol BS2 0UY

Below here the tidal Avon bypasses the Floating Harbour. It is possible to view the dam and weir from along Feeder Road, but the best views can be had from Whitby Road across the other side of the Avon.

How to get there
By road: From central Bristol follow the A4 past Bristol Temple Meads a short distance to the traffic lights before Bath Bridge. Turn left down Cattle Market

1. Clifton Suspension Bridge
2. South Entrance Lock
3. Swing bridge
4. Underfall dam
5. SS Great Britain
6. Brunel House
7. City museum
8. Bristol University library
9. Brunel statue
10. Industrial Museum
11. Temple Meads station

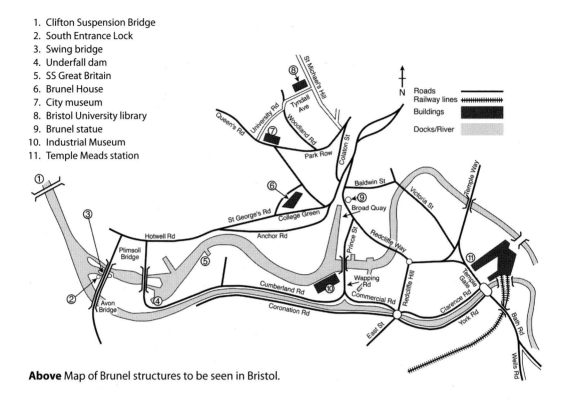

Above Map of Brunel structures to be seen in Bristol.

Road, under the railway bridge and turn right into Feeder Road. Continue along the road for one mile, past the traffic lights at the junction with Netham Road, then turn right down Whitby Road, almost doubling back on yourself but on the other side of the Avon.

Avon Bridge
Whitby Road, Bristol

This beautiful triple-arch railway bridge across the Avon is now all but hidden from view behind steel railway bridges on either side. However, with a bit of scrambling in the grass and reeds to the right of Whitby Road just before the railway crosses over the road, a matter of 100yd further down from the Netham Dam and Weir it is possible to see Brunel's fine stone bridge hiding behind the new steel structures.

How to get there
By road: Directions as for the Netham Dam and Weir.

Temple Meads Old Station Engine Shed

Station Approach, Bristol BS1 6QH
(occupying offices in station frontage)

Information
Tel 0117 903 1100 or see website (www.engine-shed.co.uk).

Left 'Great Western' legend on the frontage of the old Temple Meads station building. *Author*

Brunel's Old Station

The Passenger Shed, Station Approach, Bristol BS1 6QH (occupying the old trainshed)

Information

Tel 08446 622 970 or see website (www.brunels-old-station.co.uk).

Parking

NCP Temple Gate (opposite), plus limited short-stay on station approach.

How to get there

On foot: Leave Temple Meads station booking hall and walk down station approach where you will find the old station buildings on the right-hand side.

Left Opposite the approach road to Bristol Temple Meads station is the 'Reckless Engineer' public house. *Author*

Brunel's SS *Great Britain*

Great Western Dockyard, Gas Ferry Road, Bristol BS1 6TY

Brunel's SS *Great Britain* is a fully accessible all-weather attraction. Tickets allow for unlimited visits for a year and include audio tours. Visitors are also able to pre-book tickets from the SS *Great Britain* online shop. Refreshments are in the café.

Information

Tel 0117 926 0680 or see website (www.ssgreatbritain.org).

Opening times

Daily, 10.00–16.30 during GMT, 17.30 during BST. Last entry one hour before closing. Closed 24 and 25 December and on the first Monday after each New Year bank holiday.

Parking

Use the pay-and-display car park next to Brunel's SS *Great Britain* (or nearby on-street parking). Alternatively visitors can travel by train, harbour ferry, bike or bus.

The Brunel Institute

Great Western Dockyard, Gas Ferry Road, Bristol BS1 6TY

The Brunel Institute is a world-class conservation and education centre alongside Brunel's SS *Great Britain*. It comprises a conservation suite and archive, major reference library, lecture theatre and seminar rooms, education space, teaching offices and a new ticket and reception area serving the whole site. In collaboration with the University of Bristol, the Institute safely displays and makes accessible the SS *Great Britain* Trust Collection, including more than 6,000 maritime books, 2,500 ship plans and 35,000 maritime photographs, as well as diaries and personal letters relating to passengers and crew of the SS *Great Britain*.

How to gain access to the collection

Access to the Brunel Institute is free of charge; no ticket to the SS *Great Britain* is required. To see the collection or use the David MacGregor Library you will need to bring a form of identification which is less than three months old, and shows your current address, such as a driving licence or utility bill. Mobile phone bills are not acceptable. Booking is not required, but if you are visiting in order to see a particular object or section of the collections, please contact the Curator of Library and Archive in advance by telephone on 0117 926 0680 or see website (www.ssgreatbritain.org/brunelinstitute).

Underfall Dam

Underfall Boatyard, Cumberland Road, Bristol BS1 6XG

Following the restoration of its slipway and buildings in the 1990s, the Underfall Yard was set up as a working boatyard with a number of maritime-related workshops and small businesses. Visitors are welcome and the yard can be found at the western end of the city's floating harbours. This is a working boatyard, so please take due care when walking through.

Information

Telephone the yard manager (0117 929 3250) or see website (www. underfallboatyard.co.uk).

Parking

Use Maritime Heritage Centre car park.

How to get there

By car or on foot: As for SS *Great Britain* but continue along Cumberland Road after the Gas Ferry Road turning for about ⅛ mile, where you will see the Underfall Yard further along on the right.

Cumberland Basin

South Entrance Lock and Swivel Bridge, Bristol BS1 6XL

Information

See website (www.brunelsotherbridge.org.uk).

Parking

Use free car park beneath the flyover.

How to get there

By car or on foot: After the turning to the SS *Great Britain* and Gas Ferry Road, continue along Cumberland Road for about ¼ mile until the road bears to the right. Then take the turning that veers off sharply to the right into Avon Crescent. Continue a short distance to a mini roundabout then turn left into Brunel Lock Road. The car park is adjacent to this road on the right, beneath the flyover. Brunel's South Entrance Lock and swivel bridge are a short distance beyond the big Avon Bridge that crosses overhead from left to right.

Clifton Suspension Bridge

Bridge Road, Clifton Down, Bristol BS8 3PA

Pedestrians may cross the bridge for free but car drivers must pay a modest toll.

Information

For guided tours tel 0117 973 8008 or see website (www.cliftonbridge.org.uk)

Parking

On-street in Sion Place and Gloucester Row.

How to get there

By road: Along Portway or Hotwell Road, turn up Bridge Valley Road and then right at top. Follow signs to bridge; alternatively, from Whiteladies Road to Blackboy Hill, turn left on reaching The Downs.

By bus: From Bristol Temple Meads station and city centre.

Left These 100-or-more-year-old gouge-marks in the metal of the swivel bridge were made by craft pushing against it to make it open more quickly. *Author*

Below There are several memorial plaques and inscriptions to be found on Clifton Suspension Bridge. This one is attached to the pier on the Clifton Down side. *Author*

Bristol City Museum & Art Gallery

Queens Road, Bristol BS8 1RL

Paintings, prints, drawings and photographs relating to the GWR, PS *Great Western* and SS *Great Britain* (including scale line drawings by William Patterson of the hulls of both ships, and 25 engravings for the latter of the engine and hull details), and the Clifton Suspension Bridge. Much material is not on public display but can be viewed by prior appointment with the Curator of Technology.

Opening times

Monday to Friday, 10.00–17.00; Saturday, Sunday and bank-holiday Mondays, 10.00–18.00. Admission free.

Information

Tel 0117 922 3571 or see website (www.bristol-city.gov.uk/museums).

Parking

In adjacent streets (meter), West End and Trenchard Street car parks.

How to get there

On foot: From city centre, via College Green to top of Park Street.

By bus: Frequent services from Temple Meads station and city centre.

Brunel House

St George's Road, Bristol BS1 5UY (façade only)

Designed by R.S. Pope in collaboration with Brunel to accommodate passengers travelling from London to New York by steam train and ship. Only the façade remains today, as part of Bristol City Council's new offices for its departments of Engineering, Planning and Environmental Health.

How to get there

On foot: Situated behind City Hall (formerly the Council House) on College Green, with access from Park Street.

By bus: As for museum.

Brunel statue

Temple Back East, Temple Quay, Bristol BS1 6DX

(outside the Bristol & West Building Society headquarters)

Parking

In adjacent streets (meter) and city centre car parks (charges apply).

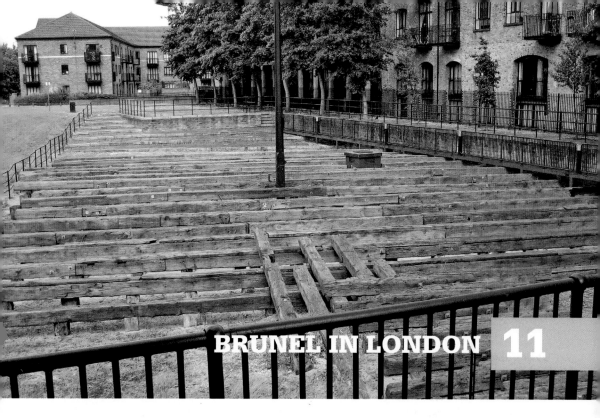

How to get there

By road: Because of traffic congestion in Central London and the suburbs as well as the Congestion Charge scheme it is advisable for your own and your passengers' sanity to park your car on the outskirts of the city and take a bus or Underground train to visit the places you wish. Buy a one-day All Zones Travelcard, available from most London-area rail and London Underground stations, or from roadside machines at most bus stops, which will allow you unlimited travel on the city's buses, tubes and trains. A mobile phone with GPS and a London *A-Z Street Atlas and Index* (Geographers' A-Z Map Co), obtainable from London news agents and station news kiosks, will also be an invaluable aid to your visit.

Above *Great Eastern* launch ramps at Millwall. *Neddyseagoon*

Right Map of Brunel-related locations in London.

1. Kensall Green cemetery
2. Paddington station
3. Science museum
4. Westminster Abbey
5. Duke Street
6. Brunel Statue
7. Thames Tunnel and Brunel engine house
8. Great Eastern launched here
9. National Maritime Museum

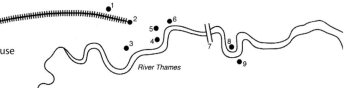

N

River Thames

By rail: Frequent main-line services from most points nationwide into London's principal termini, which are well served by Tube and bus services.

By coach: Frequent express coach and bus services from most points nationwide to Victoria Coach Station, Buckingham Palace Road, London SW1. The coach station is a 300yd walk to the Victoria, District and Circle lines.

Memorials and statuary

Statue of Isambard Brunel (standing)

At junction of Temple Place and Victoria Embankment, WC2R 0RN

Sculpted by Baron Carlo Marochetti. Born in Turin in 1805, Marochetti trained in Paris and Rome, settled in Paris and came to London in 1848 after the revolution against the *Ancien Régime*. Patronised by Queen Victoria and Prince Albert, he also executed statues of Queen Victoria and the Duke of Wellington. He died in 1867.

How to get there
Underground: Temple (Circle and District lines).

Right Carlo Marochetti's imposing statue of Brunel can be found in London on the Victoria Embankment at its junction with Temple Place, just beyond Waterloo Bridge heading east towards the City. *Author*

Statue of Isambard Brunel (seated)

Paddington station concourse, W2 6LH

Sculpted by John Doubleday (1982).

How to get there
Underground: Paddington (Circle, District, Bakerloo and Hammersmith & City lines).

ISAMBARD KINGDOM BRUNEL
CIVIL ENGINEER
BORN 1806 DIED 1859

Stained-glass window

Westminster Abbey, SW1A 2JR

Designed by Norman Shaw, the window was erected by his family in 1863 in the third bay from the west on the north side of the nave. It was moved to the south side of the nave in 1952. The inscription reads: In memory of Isambard Kingdom Brunel, civil engineer, born April 9 1806, departed this life September 15 1859'.

The window itself comprises two lights each of which measures 23ft 6in high by 4ft wide, surmounted by a quatrefoil opening 6ft 6in across. Over the inscription are four allegorical figures, two in each light, representing fortitude, justice, faith and charity. The upper part of the window consists of six panels divided by a patternwork of lilies and pomegranates. The left-hand light portrays scenes from the Old Testament. From top to bottom: Zerubbabel builds the second Temple; Hilkiah finds the Book of the Law in the Temple; Solomon dedicates the Temple. The right-hand light portrays scenes from the New Testament. From top to bottom: the disciples show Christ the buildings of the Temple; Christ sits in the midst of the doctors in the Temple; Simeon blesses Christ in the Temple.

Design of the window was placed in the hands of Norman Shaw, of the firm Nesfield & Shaw, Architects, who prepared the general design, arranged the scale of the various figures and designed the ornamental patternwork. The figure subjects were drawn by Henry Holyday and the whole design was executed by Messrs Heaton, Butler & Boyne, of Garrick Street, Covent Garden.

Opening times

Daily, 09.30–15.30; admission charges apply.

Information

Tel 0207 222 5152 or see website (www.westminster-abbey.org).

How to get there

Underground: Westminster (Circle and District lines).

Brunel family tomb

Kensal Green (All Souls') Cemetery, Harrow Road, W10 4RA

Situated on the Harrow Road (A404), sandwiched between the main lines from Euston and Paddington and the Grand Union Canal (Paddington branch). Kensal Green was London's first private cemetery to be licensed by Act of Parliament, in 1832, to relieve the chronic and insanitary overcrowding of the city's churchyards. The Brunel family grave is located about halfway along the Centre Avenue on the left-hand side before the pathways fork.

Opening times

Monday–Saturday 09.00–17.00 (09.00–18.00 in summer), Sunday 10.00–17.00; admission free.

Information

Tel 0208 969 0152 or see website (www. kensalgreencemetery.com).

How to get there

By road: The entrance to the cemetery is in Harrow Road, only 15min drive from the West End via Edgware Road and 5min

from the M40/Westway via Scrubs Lane.
By bus: Services 18 (Harrow Road) and
52 (Ladbroke Grove/Kilburn Lane).

By rail: Kensal Rise and Kensal Green
stations from Euston.

Underground: Kensal Green (Bakerloo
Line), turn left outside station and walk
along Harrow Road to cemetery entrance.
Also Ladbroke Grove (Hammersmith &
City Line).

Above The Brunel family grave is located at Kensal
Green Cemetery in West London. Surprisingly
simple and unassuming in its design, the grave
is easily missed among the many more elaborate
examples of Victorian funerary architecture. An
inscription beneath the name of Marc Brunel could
equally apply to his son Isambard: 'He has raised his
own monument by his public works'. *Author*

Locations with Brunel connections

18 Duke Street (site of)
St James's, SW1

The Brunel family home and Isambard's
office, situated between Piccadilly and
Pall Mall, adjacent to St James's Park. The
house and all the street were demolished
to make way for the Colonial Office.

How to get there
Underground: Green Park (Piccadilly,
Jubilee and Victoria lines), Piccadilly
Circus (Piccadilly and Bakerloo lines).

Hungerford Bridge (site of)
WC2

Brunel's original Hungerford suspension
bridge across the Thames was dismantled
in 1862, to be replaced in 1864 with a
nine-span structure designed by Sir John
Hawkshaw. The original red-brick piers of
Brunel's pedestrian bridge remain as the
foundations for the present day Charing
Cross railway bridge, also known as
Hungerford Bridge. It is still possible to
cross the Thames by a pedestrian bridge
at this point from Victoria Embankment to
the South Bank complex, reconstructed in
2002 as the Golden Jubilee Bridges.

How to get there
Underground: Embankment (Northern,
Bakerloo, Circle and District lines).

Thames Tunnel
Rotherhithe and Wapping

Used by London Overground for its East London-line service. Wapping station, on the north bank of the Thames, is built on the site of the original tunnel shaft; Rotherhithe station on the south bank is a short distance to the south of the original tunnel shaft. The portals of the tunnel can be seen at Wapping from the southern end of the platform, but at Rotherhithe they are hidden along an access tunnel and are only just visible to view.

How to get there
By rail: Rotherhithe and Wapping stations (London Overground East London line).

Great Eastern launch ramps (site of)
Masthouse Terrace, Napier Avenue, E14

Although no longer in existence, the site on which the *Great Eastern* was built and from which she was launched has been redeveloped since the 19th century. The riverside areas off West Ferry Road, Millwall, and the Burrel's Wharf development, off the A1206 Ferry Road, occupy the approximate site of the yard. Thames clippers will take you to the original launch ramps, now landscaped into gardens by the river pier. The information board, timbers and a very large chain are not visible from the river, so disembark at Masthouse Terrace on your way to Greenwich or before turning back for the City.

How to get there
Bus and boat: Service C10 from Rotherhithe station to the Hilton, then Hilton Hotel river ferry to Canary Wharf Pier, then Thames clipper to Masthouse Terrace Pier. The launch ramps are 10 paces away.

Train, walk and boat: London Overground from Rotherhithe to Surrey Quays; then, after a 15min walk to Greenland Pier, it's one stop east to Masthouse Terrace Pier on the Thames clipper.

Underground and bus: Jubilee Line from Canada Water to Canary Wharf, then bus D3, D7 or 135 to Westferry Road (St Edmund's School), a few yards from the launch site.

Bus and foot tunnel: Service 188 from Canada Water to Greenwich, walk through the foot tunnel to Island Gardens and then 10min upstream.

Train and bus: London Overground through the Thames Tunnel to Wapping. At Wapping take bus service D3 (every 10min Mon-Sat, every 15min Sunday) to Westferry Road (St Edmunds School), a few yards from the launch site.

Train and DLR: London Overground through the Thames Tunnel to Shadwell. At Shadwell take the Docklands Light Railway across the Isle of Dogs to Island Gardens, then a 10min walk upstream.

Museums and exhibitions

The Brunel Museum

Railway Avenue, Rotherhithe, SE16 4LF

The Brunel Museum is housed in Marc Brunel's engine house and commemorates Isambard's first and last projects: the first underwater tunnel and the first modern ocean liner. A permanent exhibition inside the engine house tells the dramatic story of the building and subsequent history of the Thames Tunnel, complemented by a representative selection of original artefacts. When the Thames Tunnel was opened in 1843, Sir Marc Brunel's Rotherhithe shaft was transformed into the Rotherhithe Grand Entrance Hall. Millions of visitors descended the impressive staircases to visit one of the great wonders of the Victorian age. The Grand Entrance Hall was closed to the public for 150 years but can be visited today on one of the regular tours organised by the Brunel Museum. The Brunel Museum is close to the construction and launch site of Brunel's last project, the *Great Eastern*. You can reach the site by boat, and the best way is to take one of the museum's weekly tours organised in partnership with London Walks.

Opening times

10.00–17.00 seven days a week, plus regular late-night openings. Guided walking tours Tuesdays 18.15 and Sundays 10.45. Guided boat tours Saturdays and Thursdays 10.45. Admission charges apply, with concessions.

Information
Tel 0207 231 3840 or E-mail (info@brunel-museum.org.uk).

How to get there
Underground: Bermondsey or Canada Water on the Jubilee Line and 10min walk, or change at Canada Water for London Overground and Rotherhithe station.

DLR: Shadwell, then East London line.

By train: Rotherhithe London Overground station is 100yd away.

By bus: Service 381 and C10 stop outside Rotherhithe station. Services 1 and 188 stop at Canada Water.

National Maritime Museum

Romney Road, Greenwich, SE10 9NF

Model of *Great Britain*, paintings and prints of Brunel's steamships.

Opening times
10.00–17.00, seven days a week; open all year round except 24–26 December (admission free).

Information
Tel 0208 858 4422 or see website (www.rmg.co.uk).

How to get there
By rail: From Charing Cross, Waterloo or London Bridge to Maze Hill.

DLR: Cutty Sark.

Pumphouse Educational Museum

Lavender Pond and Nature Park, Lavender Road, Rotherhithe, SE16 5DZ

The museum is housed in a building which originally contained dock machinery and tells the story of Rotherhithe and its people by means of a unique collection of objects found on the Thames foreshore. The Pumphouse Educational Museum, surrounded by a nature park and pond, organises educational visits for schools in conjunction with the teacher to link projects to National Curriculum Guidelines. Local history walks are organised from nearby Tower Bridge to Pumphouse to Durands Wharf (opposite Canary Wharf) with themes which can relate to the Brunels, *e.g.* the River Thames, the Victorians, and river transport and trade.

Opening times

Weekdays 10.00–16.00; closed at weekends. Admission free. Bookings by appointment.

Information

Tel 0207 231 2976 or see website (www.thepumphouse.org.uk)

How to get there

By train: London Bridge station; London Overground to Rotherhithe.

By bus: Services 225 and 381.

DLR: Surrey Quays.

The Science Museum

Exhibition Road, South Kensington, SW7 2DD

Exhibits relating to the GWR, sectional model of the Thames Tunnel, model of the Tunnelling Shield, models of the *Great Western*, *Great Britain* and *Great Eastern*, sectional models of the *Great Britain*'s engines and the *Great Eastern*'s paddle engines.

Opening times

Seven days a week, 10.00–18.00. Open all year except 24–26 December. Admission free.

Information

Tel 0870 870 4868 (or 0207 942 4000) or see website (www.sciencemuseum.org.uk).

How to get there

Underground: South Kensington (Circle and District lines).

12 BRUNEL ELSEWHERE IN GREAT BRITAIN

Berkshire

Thames Bridge

**Barry Avenue, Windsor, Berks,
SL4 5JB**

Wrought-iron bowstring girder railway
bridge, the earliest surviving example of
this type by Brunel and the world's oldest
wrought-iron bridge still in regular use.

How to get there

By road: M4 motorway Jct 6, A332 to
Windsor (2 miles). At junction with A308
turn left into Maidenhead Road, then left
again into Vansittart Road. There are a
number of car parks along the riverfront
from where access to the bridge can be
gained via the riverside gardens and
pleasure ground.

By rail: Main-line or suburban services
from London (Paddington) to Slough,
connecting service to Windsor & Eton
Central; suburban services from London
(Waterloo) to Windsor & Eton Riverside.

Sonning Cutting

**London Road, Woodley, Berks,
RG6 1BE**

Two-mile railway cutting through Sonning
Hill, with three road over-bridges.

How to get there

By road: M4 motorway Jct 10, A329(M) and
A3290 towards Reading. At junction with A4
turn right onto A4 (eastbound), which

Above A First Great Western HST from Paddington to Hereford passes through Sonning Cutting at speed on its approach to Reading. *Ken Brunt*

crosses Sonning Cutting a mile east of the junction. From here it is possible to see the cutting itself and Brunel's triple-arch brick-built bridge, as well as the metal-arch bridge that replaced his original timber structure. Duffield Road Bridge, ¾ mile up the line towards London, is a favourite with railway photographers, but Butts Hill Road offers safer parking opportunities; continue east along the A4 to the next roundabout, turn right into Pound Lane and follow this around to the right to cross the cutting.

Gatehampton (Basildon) railway bridge
Lower Basildon, Berks, RG8 9ND

Triple-arch brick railway bridge carrying the Great Western main line across the River Thames.

How to get there
By road: From Reading centre take A329 west to junction with B4009 at Great Streatley. Turn right crossing the Thames into Goring. On foot, follow the river towpath for about a mile to the bridge. From the M4 motorway leave at Jct 12 and take A340 to Pangbourne, then follow directions as above.

Buckinghamshire

Maidenhead Bridge
(also known as Maidenhead Viaduct)
River Road, Taplow, Bucks, SL6 0BB

Twin-arch brick railway bridge carrying the Great Western main line across the River Thames.

How to get there
By road: M4 motorway Jct 7, then left to Maidenhead at Jct 7a with A4. On Bridge Road, shortly before A4 crosses the river, turn left down towards the industrial estate. The bridge is now about ¼ mile ahead of you.

Devon

Brunel Tower
The Strand, Starcross, Exeter EX6 8PR

Preserved pumping station building used to house air pumps for use by Brunel's Atmospheric Railway. Now used as a boat house by Starcross Fishing & Cruising Club. Visible from the road or railway station in Starcross.

How to get there
By road: M5 motorway Jct 30, then A379 for 9 miles to Starcross, on the west side of the Exe estuary.

By rail: First Great Western from Bristol Temple Meads, or South West Trains from London (Waterloo) to Exeter St Davids, then restricted local service to Starcross; check with National Rail Enquiries (tel 08457 48 49 50 or see website – www.nationalrail.co.uk). Adjacent to Starcross railway station.

By bus and coach: Express coach links to Exeter, then local bus (service 2 from bus station) to Starcross.

Watcombe Park and Brunel Manor

Teignmouth Road, Torquay TQ1 4SF

Intended by Brunel to be his retirement home; plots of land were bought, but the house was not started until after his death. Various designers advised him on landscaping and planting, and the arboretum contains many fine trees. All that remains of the planned approach are cobbles for carriage wheels. The house is now called Brunel Manor and is maintained by the Woodlands House of Prayer Trust as a Christian holiday, retreat and conference centre. It is not open to the public.

Millbay Dock

Brunel Way, Millbay, Plymouth PL1 3EF

Brunel-designed dock, brought back to life as the 171-berth King Point Marina.

How to get there

By road: Plymouth is easily reached from all parts of the UK. Take the A38 Devon Expressway to Plymouth, then A374 through city following signs for Channel Ferry, Stonehouse and King Point Marina.

By rail: First Great Western from London, Bristol and Virgin Trains from the North to Plymouth. Bus link to Mill Bay Docks.

Royal Albert Bridge

Saltash, Cornwall, PL12 4GT

Tubular iron railway suspension bridge carrying the Great Western main line across the River Tamar.

How to get there

By road: M5 motorway to Exeter, A38 to Plymouth, B3413 to Saltash.

By rail: First Great Western from London and Bristol and Virgin Trains from the North to Plymouth. A frequent bus service from outside the railway station crosses the Tamar road bridge. Alight at the stop after crossing the bridge.

Middlesex

Wharncliffe Viaduct

Southall, Mddx, UB1 3ER

Brick railway viaduct, almost 900ft long with eight semi-elliptical arches, carrying the Great Western main line across the Brent Valley.

How to get there

By road: M4 motorway Jct 1, then A406 Gunnersbury Avenue towards Acton for 1½ miles, then left onto A4020 Uxbridge Road for 2 miles. As you pass the junction with the A3002 Lower Boston Road on the left, the viaduct can be seen away to the right, off the Uxbridge Road, crossing Churchfields recreation ground.

By rail: Suburban service from London Paddington to Hanwell. From Station

Approach turn into Station Road and follow to Broadway, then turn right and follow the road as it turns into Uxbridge Road.

Oxfordshire

Moulsford railway bridge

The Street, Moulsford, Oxon, OX10 9EX or Ferry Lane, South Stoke, Oxon, RG8 0JP

Four-arch brick railway bridge (known locally as 'Four Arches Bridge') carrying the Great Western main line across the River Thames.

How to get there

By road: The same route as for Basildon, but turn left at junction with B4009 and follow the road to South Stoke. Turn left into village passing beneath the railway bridge and follow the road until the river is reached. Walk north for ½ mile along the eastern towpath to the bridge.

Sunderland

Monkwearmouth Dock

Monkwearmouth, Sunderland, SR6 0PW

Brunel-designed dock, although there is little left to see except dock walls. Now redeveloped as a marina and housing complex.

How to get there

By road: A690 from Durham; A1018 from Stockton and South Shields. From the city centre cross the River Wear by Wearmouth Bridge, then turn right into the A183 Dame Dorothy Street and continue for one mile, passing the junction on the left to Roker Avenue. The dock is now on your right.

By rail: From principal stations to Sunderland, then by local bus or walk.

By bus: From Sunderland bus station (service 700) to Sunderland Marina.

Wiltshire

Box Tunnel (west portal)

Brunel Way, Box, Corsham, SN13 8ES

Brunel-designed 9,636ft-long railway tunnel.

How to get there

By road: A4 from Bath. On entering the village take the left fork at the traffic lights and continue through the village for 1½ miles until just before the bridge over the railway line. Turn right and park in the Bargates estate. Cross the main road and turn right, crossing the bridge, then re-cross the road to the observation point from which the tunnel can be viewed. Take care, as this is a busy road.

By bus: Bath bus station (services 271 and 272, journey time 20min). Alight at Box Post Office, then walk the 50yd to the railway bridge.

STEAM – Museum of the Great Western Railway

Fire Fly Avenue, Swindon SN2 2EY

Museum housing relics of the GWR and a collection of Brunel memorabilia.

Opening times
10.00–17.00 daily (except 24, 25 and 26 December and 1 January); admission charges apply, with concessions.

Information
Tel 01793 466646 or see website (www.steam-museum.org.uk)

How to get there
By road: Follow the brown tourist signs for Swindon Designer Outlet and STEAM or the 'M' (museum) signs. STEAM is on the historic Churchward site in Rodbourne, northwest of Swindon town centre. Enter 'Kemble Drive, Swindon' into your sat nav to find it.

By rail: Swindon is on the line from London (Paddington) to Bristol, and STEAM is just 10min walk from Swindon station (signposted).

Parking
Car parking is strictly limited to the nearby Swindon Designer Outlet car parks. Visitors can obtain a free parking ticket from STEAM Reception. For disabled and coach parking tel 01793 466626 or 01793 466637. Note there is no visitor parking in front of STEAM.

Yorkshire

National Railway Museum

Leeman Road, York YO26 4XJ

National railway collection, including a collection of Brunel memorabilia.

Opening times
10.00–18.00 daily. Admission free.

Information
Tel (Mon–Fri 09.00–17.00) 08448 153139 (general enquiries) or 01904 611112 (research enquiries) or see website (www.nrm.org.uk).

How to get there
By road: A1036 from Leeds and Scarborough; A59 from Harrogate. From the city centre cross over the River Ouse by Lendal Bridge and turn right into Leeman Road. Continue along the road, passing under the railway bridge. The museum is on your right.

By rail: Main-line services from London (King's Cross), Bristol and Edinburgh. Leaving station, turn left into Station Road, immediately left into Station Rise, then into Leeman Road.

Wales

Chepstow Railway Bridge

Mount Pleasant, Chepstow, NP16 7EQ

The original railway suspension bridge was replaced in 1962 with a welded truss bridge. Only the piers beneath the land spans and the southwest abutment remain of Brunel's original design.

How to get there

By road: Follow the A48 northeast from Chepstow towards Tidenham and Woolaston. The main road crosses the River Wye parallel to the railway bridge. It is possible to view the bridge from the banks of the Wye.

Loughor Railway Viaduct

Llwchwr, Swansea SA4 6TP

The last vestiges of Brunel's 18-span timber trestle viaduct were replaced in 2013 with a new steel viaduct capable of supporting two tracks. However, five trestles from the 1909 structure have been retained in the estuary as a reminder of the old viaduct – four to the west and one to the east.

How to get there

By road: A484 west from Swansea to Llanelli. The A484 road bridge runs parallel to the railway viaduct as it crosses the Loughor estuary. A pavement borders the main road, from where the viaduct can be viewed.

Briton Ferry Dock

Briton Ferry, Neath, SA11 2HZ

Preserved Brunel-designed dock with dockside power house, dock walls and half of inner floating dock, quoins and dock gate. Awaiting further redevelopment.

How to get there

By road: M4 motorway Jct 41, then A48 for 5 miles; alternatively A48 from Cardiff or A483 from Swansea.

By rail: First Great Western from London Paddington and Bristol Parkway to Swansea, change for local rail service to Neath, then local bus or taxi to Briton Ferry.

By bus or coach: Express coach links to Swansea. Local bus service to Briton Ferry from Swansea's City Bus Station (service 157 to Neath).

Scotland

Balmoral Bridge

Crathie, Aberdeenshire, AB35 5TL

At Crathie there is a somewhat plain-looking iron girder bridge that spans the River Dee, linking the church and car park to Balmoral.

How to get there

By road: Follow the B976 west from Ballater to Crathie. The road crosses the Balmoral Bridge to join the A93 to Crathie.

Bibliography

Books

J. Adams and P. Elkin: *Isambard Kingdom Brunel* (Jarrold, 1988)

P. Beaver: *The Big Ship: Brunel's Great Eastern – A Pictorial History* (Hugh Evelyn, London)

D. Beckett: *Brunel's Britain* (David & Charles, 1980)

G. Biddle: *Great Railway Stations of Britain* (David & Charles, 1986)

J.C. Bourne: *The History & Description of the Great Western Railway* (David Bogue, 1846)

I. Brunel: *The Life of Isambard Kingdom Brunel, Civil Engineer* (Longman, Green & Co, 1870)

R.A. Buchanan and M. Williams: *Brunel's Bristol* (Redcliffe Press, 1982)

J. Christopher: *The Lost Works of Isambard Kingdom Brunel* (Amberley Publishing, 2011)

R.A. Cooke: *Atlas of the Great Western Railway 1947* (Wild Swan Publications Ltd, 1988)

B.K. Cooper: *Great Western Railway Handbook* (Ian Allan, 1986)

J. Culbertson and T. Randall: *Permanent Londoners – An Illustrated Guide to the Cemeteries of London* (Robson Books, 1991)

C.H. Ellis: *Railway Art* (Ash & Grant, 1977)

G. Farr: *The SS Great Western – The First Atlantic Liner* (Bristol Historical Association, 1988)

D. Griffiths: *Brunel's 'Great Western'* (Patrick Stephens, 1985)

E.J. Hobsbawm: *Industry and Empire* (Pelican, 1980)

E. Jenkins (Ed): *Neath and District – A Symposium* (1974)

G.P. Jones and A. G. Pool: *A Hundred Years of Economic Development* (Duckworth, 1966)

B. Lake: British Newspapers: *A History and Guide for Collectors* (Sheppard Press, 1984)

B. Lavery: *SS Great Britain Enthusiasts' Manual* (Haynes Publishing, 2012)

J. Lord and J. Southam: *The Floating Harbour – A Landscape* History of Bristol City Docks (Redcliffe Press, 1983)

A. Mathewson and D. Laval: *Brunel's Tunnel … and where it led* (Brunel Exhibition Rotherhithe, 1992)

P. Mathias: *The First Industrial Nation* (Methuen, 1969)

G. Milburn and S. Miller: *Sunderland: River, Town and People – A History from the 1780s* (Sunderland Borough Council, 1990 [second edition])

C. Morgan: *Briton Ferry (Llansawel)* (Cliff Morgan, 1977)

C. Morgan: *A Pictorial Record of Briton Ferry (Llansawel)* (Cliff Morgan, 1979)

C. Morgan: *Briton Ferry Notes* (Cliff Morgan, 1994)

J.F. Nicholls and J. Taylor: *Bristol Past and Present Vol III: Civil and Modern History* (J.W. Arrowsmith, Bristol, 1882)

R. Powell: *Brunel's Kingdom: Photography and the Making of History* (Watershed, 1985)

A. Pugsley: *The Works of Isambard Kingdom Brunel* (Cambridge University Press, 1980)

L.T.C. Rolt: *Isambard Kingdom Brunel* (Penguin, 1989 edition)

R. Tames: *Lifelines 1: Isambard Kingdom Brunel* (Shire Publications, 1992)

A. Vaughan: *Isambard Kingdom Brunel* (John Murray, 1991)

Chambers' Biographical Dictionary (New Edition, 1961)

The Concise Dictionary of National Biography, Part I (Oxford University Press, 1906)

SS Great Britain Guide (SS Great Britain Trading, 1992)

Newspapers, magazines and periodicals

The Cambrian (1861)

The Illustrated London News (various issues, 1843–64)

Neath Guardian (1990)

Swansea Evening Post (1989 and 1992)

The Times (various issues)

Western Mail (1990)

Websites

British Listed Buildings (www.britishlistedbuildings.co.uk) – an online database of buildings and structures that are listed as being of special architectural and historic interest.